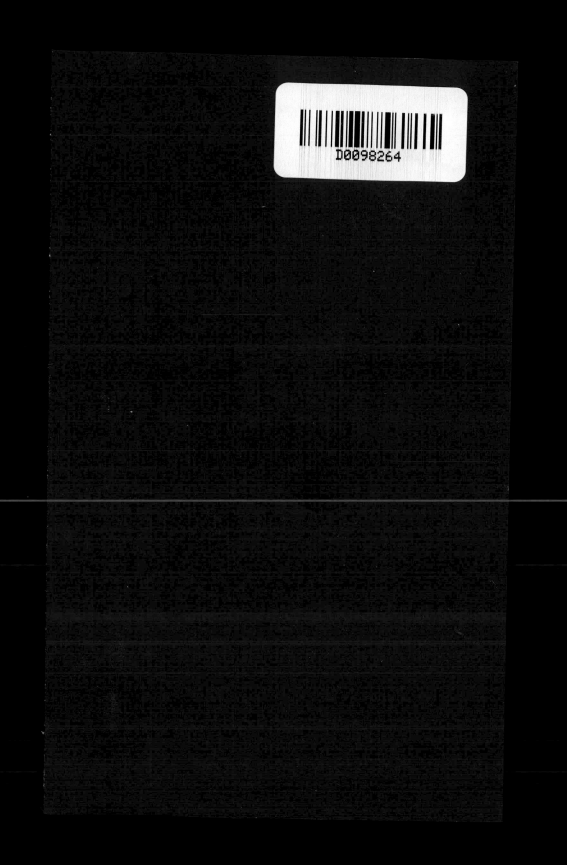

ULTIMATE QUESTIONS

Ultimate Questions

Bryan Magee

PRINCETON UNIVERSITY PRESS

Princeton and Oxford

Library of Congress Cataloging-in-Publication Data

Magee, Bryan.
Ultimate questions / Bryan Magee.
pages cm
Includes bibliographical references and index.
ISBN 978-0-691-17065-7 (hardcover : alk. paper) 1. Human beings.
2. Philosophical anthropology. 3. Ontology. 4. Philosophy. I. Title.
BD450.M255 2016
128—dc23
2015034960

British Library Cataloging-in-Publication Data is available

This book has been composed in ITC Galliard

Printed on acid-free paper. ∞

Printed in the United States of America

1 3 5 7 9 10 8 6 4 2

CONTENTS

ULTIMATE QUESTIONS

Time and Space

WHAT WE CALL CIVILISATION HAS EXISTED FOR SOME-
thing like six thousand years. We are accustomed to
thinking of this as an exceedingly long time. Some of
us have a vague outline of it in our heads. In my part
of the world this usually starts with the Old Testa-
ment of the Bible, followed or accompanied by the
rise of Greek civilisation, which was followed by the
Roman Empire—each of which lasted for hundreds
of years. Then came the thousand years of the Middle Ages. This ended with the Renaissance, which
was followed by the Reformation, followed by the
Enlightenment, then by the Industrial Revolution

and the Romantic Era—and then on to the modern
world and our own day. Across these same immensi-
ties of time other civilisations—unknown, or mostly
unknown, to the people in my part of the world—
rose and fell on other parts of the globe's surface:
China, Japan, India, Central Asia, the Middle East,
South America, Mexico. We think of these vast historical changes as happening in only-just-moving
time—time moving in the sort of way a glacier moves.

But now consider the following. There are always
some human beings who live to be a hundred. More
do so today than ever before, but there have always
been some. I have known three quite well, two of
them public figures: the politician Emmanuel Shin-
well and the musical philanthropist Robert Mayer.
(Robert knew Brahms, who was a friend of his family
and stayed with them in Mannheim.) When Robert
was born there must have been individuals who were
then a hundred years old, whom a person could have
met and got to know in the same way as I got to
know him (or as he got to know Brahms, who died
when Robert was seventeen). When those others were
born, there must have been yet other such individuals.
And so on: one could go further and further back,
putting the lives of nameable human beings together,
end to end, without any gaps in between. It comes
as a shock to realise that the whole of civilisation
has occurred within the successive lifetimes of sixty
people—which is the number of friends I squeeze into
my living room when I have a drinks party. Twenty

people take us back to Jesus, twenty-one to Julius Caesar. Even a paltry ten take us back before 1066 and the Norman Conquest. As for the Renaissance, it is only half a dozen people away.

When one measures history by a single possible human lifetime one realises that the whole of it has been almost incredibly short. This means that historical change has been almost incredibly fast. Each of those great empires that so imposingly rose, flourished and fell did so during the overlapping lives of a handful of individuals, usually fewer than half a dozen. So we ourselves are still near the beginning of the entire story. Tomorrow will be followed by the next day, next year by the year after, next century by the century after, next millennium by the millennium after, and the year 20,000 will inevitably come, as will the year 200,000, and the year 2,000,000. It is unstoppable. In fact, as periods in the existence of our planet and other bodies in the universe go, these are short periods of time. From now on, as long as there are human beings on this or any other heavenly body, humans will have a continuous, ever-extending history that traces itself back unbrokenly to our day now and our planet here. What is going to happen to all those people—what will they do—in unending time? How in the far, far future will they think of us now, who are so near the beginning of it all, and whom they will know a lot about if they choose to? How shall we appear to them in the light of all that will have happened between us and them, in a period

many, many times as long as that between the dawn
of civilisation and today?

I can imagine some of my readers throwing their
hands up and protesting: "How can we even think
about these things? What concepts do we have for
getting hold of any of this? Surely it is self-evident
that, a mere two or three thousand years ago, ge-
niuses as great as any there have been, people like
Socrates and Plato, could not have foreseen today's
world, or almost any of the world's history between
their time and ours? What imaginings can we hope
to conjure up that are worth having about a period,
all of it still in the future, so many times as long as
that? It's a blank. We could make a few guesses about
developments in the *near* future, perhaps, but history
shows us that even those are more likely to be wrong
than right. The truth is we don't know, we cannot
know, we haven't the remotest idea. We have no choice
but to go on with our lives in the present, pushing
into that tiny little bit of the future that our "now"
slides into, without thinking about any of the things
you're saying—not because they aren't worth thinking
about (it would be wonderful if we could) but because
we have no way of thinking about them, nothing to
think about them *with*."

My answer is: I have posited nothing outside the
ordinary, everyday order of events—nothing religious,
nothing supernatural, nothing transcendental. I have
merely asked what will happen if circumstances continue exactly as they are today, and go on in this fa-

miliar way, as we expect them to do. For such a continuance *not* to occur might need the intervention
of something supernatural, say, like time stopping.
There is, it is true, a possibility that the earth will
stop, because it could be smashed to pieces in a collision with a body from outer space, or frozen into
lifelessness by the sun's cooling; but such possibilities
lie either millions (at least) of years in the future or
at the outer extremes of unlikelihood. Most are such
that the human race will get warning of them before
they occur, and may even be able to do something to
prevent their happening. For instance, nuclear weapons may turn out to be the saving of the human race.
If astronomers tell us that a huge asteroid is on a collision course with our earth, we may be able to knock
it off course with nuclear missiles and save ourselves.
The missiles would have to be far more powerful
than any we have now, but that will happen in the
normal course of events. On the other hand it is possible that the human race will destroy itself with
those same weapons, thereby bringing its history to
an end—but that is rendered unlikely by the fact that
our every movement from present into future is dom-
inated by our need to solve the problems of survival.
The most obvious likelihood is that the human race
will go on living through vast stretches of future
time but not necessarily on planet earth: people may
find somewhere better to live, or be forced into moving by the earth's becoming uninhabitable. In any
case at every point in time they will have a past that

is continuous with our past, most of which they will
know better than we know it ourselves, because information technology will have been developing during that time.

We are used to thinking of our knowledge of our
own past as capacious. Through the last thousand
years the nearer history approaches to our own day,
the more detailed it becomes. Our knowledge of the
twentieth century is unprecedentedly detailed. But we
need to remind ourselves that the knowledge we have
of the twentieth century was unknowable to anyone
living only two hundred years ago. Their location in
time sealed them off from it. To them, the twentieth
century was as blank as future centuries are to us.
Wherever in time human beings may be positioned
they know their past but not their future. Yet the
events themselves—past, present and future—are the
same for everyone, and occur in the same order. It is
emphatically not the case that, because we human beings can have little or no knowledge of future events,
those events will be vague and indefinite. It is we
who are vague and indefinite. It is our knowledge—or
rather lack of it—that is the blank. The future is full.
We just do not yet know what it is. The events that
will fill it are as concrete, factual and specific as those
that fill our past.

What we can know, and what we can understand,
is so influenced by our location in time that it is impossible for us to disentangle that influence and get a
clear look at it. It governs not only our knowledge of
our present history and our present future but even

our present knowledge of our present society. We cannot see it in perspective. Wherever we are in time almost nothing about our society—from its social structure to its physical plant, from its arts and sciences to its cookery and clothing, from its economy to its religion, from its modes of warfare to its methods of transport, from its manners and mores to its uses of language—is the same as it had been a hundred years before, or as it will be a hundred years hence. For this reason most people are as provincial in time as they are in space: they huddle down into their time and regard it as their total environment. But the opposite would be nearer the truth. Their time is about to be swept away and become nothing but a memory—and not even that for very long, but rather an ever-receding sliver of an ever-expanding history. Little of it will survive in anyone's mind. Even less will be of lasting interest, except to historians.

Nevertheless, each one of us has no choice but to live the whole of his life in his own little bit of time. That is his ration, his all. In life as we know it, time is the cruellest, the most lethal of all the forms of our limitation. In the words of a well-known hymn:

> Time, like an ever-rolling stream,
>   Bears all its sons away;
> They fly forgotten, as a dream
>   Dies at the opening day.

There is no escaping this. Within the empirical world all time will be taken away from us, and with it everything we have and are in this world.

While we are enjoying our moment our spatial movements are confined to a small space, so our limitations in that dimension too are draconian. So narrowly programmed are we biologically for a life on the surface of this planet that if we attempt to depart far from the surface, either inward (under the earth or the sea) or outward (into space), we die unless we can find some artificial way of carrying our surface environment with us. Up to now we have not got far—neither deep nor high. The only object apart from earth that humans have set foot on is the moon, which is less than 240,000 miles away. Meanwhile the already-visible universe is 1,000,000,000,000,000,000,000,000 miles across. The Astronomer Royal tells us that we must expect the not-yet-visible universe to extend beyond that by distances which—measured not in miles but in light-years—would be written "not with ten zeros, not even with a hundred, but with millions." Our solar system is the merest speck in all this. Such is the relationship between a human lifetime and the astronomical distances involved that it is unlikely that humans will ever be able to penetrate even as far as the edge of their own solar system.

When I was a graduate student at Yale I was taught that the concept of time and the concept of space are logically interdependent. We find it impossible to define time-concepts without using space-concepts in the definition, and vice versa. Since Einstein, time and space have been understood by physicists to be "inextricably interconnected," as Stephen Hawking puts it.

The interconnections are many and profound and not always easy to understand. But let us consider the following.

If I look through a telescope at a star whose light takes nearly a hundred years to reach the earth, I see that star as it was nearly a hundred years ago. For all I know it may not be in that position now: it may have exploded at some time during the last century, or it may now be in a different part of the sky. In any event what impinges on my retina is the light that left that star all those years ago. But this is no different from what happens when I look at anything else. If I look at a person in the same room as myself I see him not as he is "now" but as he was at some point in the past—namely the length of time ago that it has taken light to travel from him to me. In our ordinary lives the distances involved, and therefore the time-intervals, are so minuscule that we ignore them—in fact we are unaware of their existence. But they do exist. And this has the following consequence.

If, on the star I was talking of, there is a sentient being looking at our earth through a telescope, he sees our earth as it was nearly a hundred years ago (in our time). If his telescope is a super-powerful one which enables him to observe human movements, he could be sitting there in my "now" watching World War I being fought. He is watching not a record of the events, or some sort of re-run of them, as in a film, or anything of that sort: he is watching *them*. He is looking at the events themselves, and seeing the

same things as an officer standing on the battlefield
with a pair of field-glasses. Both of them are receiving
the same light waves travelling towards them at the
same speed, and impinging in the same way on the
lenses through which they are looking. The sentient
being with the telescope is as direct an observer of
events as the officer on the battlefield.

If, at the same time by our time, on a different star
almost two thousand light-years away, another observer is observing our earth with an even more powerful telescope, he could be watching the crucifixion
of Jesus. From a star much nearer, someone could be
directly observing the Battle of Hastings. And from a
star nearer still, someone could be watching the first
Queen Elizabeth processing through the crowded
streets of sixteenth-century London. Events not only
in human history but throughout the whole history
of the earth could be directly observed simultaneously by watchers from stars at different distances.
And there would be nothing supernatural about any
of it. We are familiar with the idea of God as a being
who sees the whole of history simultaneously, but a
group of human beings could do it if they were able
to set up appropriate observation equipment in the
right places. There would be no time-travel involved
in any of it, and no magic or miracles. They would
merely be connecting themselves up to something
that is going on all the time.

Einstein believed, on purely scientific grounds, that
there is no objective "now" as far as physics is con-

cerned, and that what counts as "now" depends on the position of the observer relative to what is observed. But if only relative to an observer can there be "now," then only relative to an observer can there be past and future. Einstein was explicit about this: he thought that the idea of pastness and futureness as existing objectively was an illusion, albeit a persistent one that has almost a stranglehold on the human mind. We can better understand the meaning of this if we reflect that every moment in the history we know was "present" for the people living in it, "future" for those who lived before it, and "past" for those who came after, yet the events and their sequence were exactly the same for everybody. This is true, says Einstein, of everything in time. Events have an order in time, so there is temporal order—it is important to understand that he is not disputing that—but in this temporal order there is no privileged moment which is "now." To put it another way, time *sequence* is objective, but the *flow of time* is not. The flow of time is a characteristic of experience. So many physicists since Einstein have followed him in this that it cannot be said to be a mystical view: it is a scientific one. Actually the philosophers got there first, with Kant; but it makes a world of difference when a philosophical conjecture acquires a scientific foundation.

So deeply mysterious is the nature of time that important aspects of it continue to be matters in live dispute among physicists. I would be foolish, not being a physicist, to attempt to argue in scientific terms for one view as against another. But the very existence of the controversy among scientists demonstrates, as I have said, that these problems exist independently of philosophy or religion; and they certainly do not have solutions in terms of common sense, or even solutions that are easily intelligible to common sense. Quite the contrary. They baffle common sense.

In some fundamental way, time and space are structural to matter, which could not exist without them. All physical objects, to exist at all, must have a location in space, and also a location in time. What is more, all material objects are ephemeral: they come into existence, are perpetually changing throughout their existence, and—whether suddenly or slowly—go out of existence. To this our bodies are no exception. As Galileo said, if we were immortal we could not be in this world. The time-span of a human body's existence sets limits to the distances through which it can move, so at any given time we may be able to make a partially informed guess as to what these may be. For instance, if it were the case that nothing could move faster than the speed of light, and no person could live longer than 200 years, then no one would be able to get more than 200 light-years away from his starting point—though of course that would not necessarily have to be the earth. Even if the speed of light is not a limiting velocity, it may well be that successive journeys in successive lifetimes will still have the effect of keeping human beings confined to a corner of their universe for aeons of time.

The way we apprehend all material objects other than ourselves is affected by their size relative to us. They range from stars millions of times the size of our earth to the constituents of sub-atomic particles. Our perspective on them differs from that of other sentient creatures, even though those creatures may have a lot in common with us, and by the measures of the universe may be similar in size to us. For instance, to us a lawn looks and feels like a carpet underfoot, but to an ant living in its grass it must seem in almost every way different. Yet the differences are of proportion, position and perspective only. Physically, all of us—not only sentient creatures but physical objects of every kind—are made of the same stuff. When any of us dies, or any physical body is destroyed, the atoms that constituted it disperse, but they do not cease to exist. Having, before our existence, been part of other solids, liquids and gases—and having then come together temporarily to constitute you and me—they will disperse again to constitute other things. All the material objects thus formed are ephemeral, are temporary arrangements. Only the atoms, or rather their constituents, are indestructible.

It is an astonishing fact, but it is a fact, that the same matter constitutes everything, like a gigantic pack of cards that are never-endingly reshuffled and redealt. As Heisenberg, who introduced the uncertainty principle into quantum mechanics, put it: "Now we know that it is always the same matter, the same various chemical compounds that may belong to any object, to minerals as well as animals or plants; also the forces that act between the different parts of matter are ultimately the same in every kind of object. . . . We have here actually the final proof for the unity of matter. All the elementary particles are made of the same substance, which we may call energy or universal matter; they are just different forms in which matter can appear." The number of years for which each particle has existed is so great that each has been part of countless billions of other objects, no doubt some of them organisms, before it was part of us. And of such an order is the number of particles needed to make up a human being—such, also, the biochemistry of human reproduction—that huge numbers of the particles that constitute each one of us have almost certainly belonged to other people. In that sense, each of us is a reincarnation. And, as I have said, each of us is only a temporary arrangement.

Hundreds of years before science had explained these things to us in terms of particles and atoms, Shakespeare seems to have grasped the essential point. (One sometimes feels he understood everything.) At one moment in *Hamlet* the Prince says (or sings) the lines

Imperious Caesar, dead and turn'd to clay,
Might stop a hole, to keep the wind away.
O, that that earth, which kept the world in awe,
Should patch a wall to expel the winter's flaw!

Earlier in the play Hamlet says to King Claudius: "A man may fish with the worm that hath eat of a king, and eat of the fish that hath fed of that worm." The King, aware that he is being needled, says: "What dost thou mean by this?" and Hamlet answers: "Nothing, but to show you how a king may go a progress through the guts of a beggar."

Every one of these perspectives needs to be absorbed into an adequate view of ourselves. And the list is nowhere near complete. How can we, buried almost invisibly as we are in the ongoing processes of the universe—each of us here for only the flicker of an eyelid—hope to know even so much as *what* there is to be understood, let alone understand it? The idea that everything is in principle comprehensible to humans—and therefore that nothing can exist that is not comprehensible to humans—is unworthy of head-space. The pioneering scientist J. S. Haldane (father of the better-known J.B.S.) was always, I believe, a materialist, and once said: "The universe is not only queerer than we suppose; it is queerer than we *can* suppose." Even the most rational of persons needs to grasp that.

When all these factors have been taken into account, it is surely clear that reality will never be intellectually mastered by humans. New discoveries are being made all the time, nonstop, and some of them require us to change our existing ideas. And there is always indefinitely more to discover. The sciences are racing ahead even during the time I am writing this book. Hardly does an enquirer get a grasp of the latest developments before the significance of them is altered by new advances. Any individual who looks at the world around him and tries to master it with his understanding is all the time having the rug pulled out from under his feet. He has scarcely finished struggling to liberate himself from the inadequacies of an earlier way of looking at things before he finds the inadequacies of the new way being exposed. There is no end to this process.

Another factor that makes it impossible to achieve intellectual mastery of the world is that nothing can be fully understood only from inside: everything needs always to be seen from outside as well. This is true of people, objects, countries, societies, institutions, belief-systems, ideas—everything. This being so, those of us engaged in this kind of pursuit already have one foot in a trap. In our attempts to understand the universe we cannot get outside the universe. In our attempts to understand the empirical world we cannot get outside the empirical world. In our attempts to understand ourselves as human beings we cannot get outside ourselves as human beings. This is not, and I hope obviously not, to say that we cannot understand anything. But it is certainly to say that we cannot understand everything.

TWO

Finding Our Bearings

FROM BEGINNINGLESS TIME, OR FROM THE BEGIN-
ning of time if time had a beginning, it was true that
in a particular year a leader called Margaret Thatcher
would emerge on that part of our planet's surface that
is now called Britain. At any moment in history when-
soever, in any place wheresoever, this statement would
have been true. But before Thatcher was born I take
it no one uttered it. Until well into the twentieth century it was a truth impossible to know. This impossibility has nothing to do with language. The truth
itself would always have been easy to state in language, and easy to understand. The ancient Romans
knew Britain, and knew of at least one formidable

leader there who was a woman, Boadicea. They also knew other leaders in distant territories who had peculiar names. So they would have been in no difficulty as far as language was concerned. The truth in question, although simple and easy to state, was not knowable.

When the future becomes past, as inevitably it will, it will be as unique and specific as our present past; and we or our descendants will know it in the same way as we know what is past now. If we knew our future now, we would have very few difficulties in talking about most of it. If doing so called on us to refer to inventions or institutions that have not yet come into existence we could usually get round this with a description. If somebody in the Middle Ages had imagined television, then as far as language goes it need not have taken him more than a few sentences to give some sort of indication of what he had in mind. He would certainly not have needed to understand it before he could talk about it. Very few of us who possess television sets and talk about what we see on them understand it—or our telephones, or our cars, or our computers. It is common for us to make legitimate and meaningful statements about things we do not understand.

With the passage of time, when statements that are now true about future events refer to them in the past, their status as truths will not have been altered. But only then will they have become knowable. And only then, in most cases, will it be possible for us to formulate them in language. By "possible" here I mean possible in practice, there never having been any obstacle as far as language was concerned. And when those parts of the future become past they will appear, and be, no more than extensions of the past we now have; and their character as history will be continuous with that past, in the same way as everything that was past up to now was at one time future, and its character was then continuous with our present future.

The fact that truths about future events are true now, and have always been true, leads some people into the mistaken belief that, for this to be so, the future must be determined. Such people are confusing linguistic reference with causal connection. If at some point in future time I am going to make an unprepared, unpressured, free and quite arbitrary decision to do a particular thing, then it is true now that I shall do that. A present truth about a future free decision is no differently true from a present truth about a future anything else. There are people who are determinists, but I am not one of them, and determinism is no part of anything I have to say.

Truths about the future are far from being the only ones that press upon human beings in all their detailed reality while being transcendental and unknowable. (What I mean by "transcendental" is existent without being a fact in the empirical world: for example, value, or beauty.) One of them in particular fascinates me, the existence of the visual world for the congenitally blind. This gives us the clearest indication we can get of the nature of our relationship to what is transcendental for all of us. For those who are sighted the visual world is simply there, but a congenitally blind person cannot apprehend this kind of "there," he can get it only second-hand from the rest of us. Otherwise what would it, or could it, refer to? Where is "there" for him? Although he possesses all, or almost all, the language he would need to describe it, he is not able to do so, because he cannot apprehend it. The rest of us are also in this position with regard to inapprehensible reality: it exists, and is all around us (and touches us, so to speak, indeed includes us), but we cannot apprehend it. There is nothing irrational or religious, still less occult, about this.

Examples I have given up to this point are expressible in language because what is inapprehensible by some is apprehensible by others: the visual world, inapprehensible to the congenitally blind, is apprehensible to the sighted; and the history of what is still future, inapprehensible to everyone up to now, becomes moment by moment apprehensible, as the future modulates into the past. In both cases there is human experience somewhere that corresponds to reality, and this makes possible its description in language by the use of empirical concepts that derive from experience. However, with aspects of reality that can never be experienced by anybody, there can be no such concepts, and therefore no such descriptive utterance.

Schopenhauer was partly right when he said that if a creature with higher powers than us were to tell us about aspects of reality that lie outside all possibility of human experience, we would not understand what he was talking about. The reason I say "partly" right is that it would be a disclosure of epoch-making magnitude if that creature were to say: "There is no creator god, but when you die you will not be wholly annihilated, you will partake of existence in a form different from any you are now able to conceptualise." Where Schopenhauer is right, however, and very importantly right, is that no words any such creature could go on to utter would make it possible for us to form any determinate conception of such an existence. If any of my readers doubts this he should remember that although we can tell the congenitally blind that there are such things as colours, no words of ours will ever enable them to conceptualise actual colours. They know from us that colours exist, but they cannot envisage them. The crucial distinction here, as so often, is between "knowing that" and "knowing." The truth of a momentous fact may sometimes be conveyed, while what it would be like to experience it remains forever unintelligible.

We can know (and I think we do know) that aspects of reality exist that are permanently outside the possibility of human apprehension. We can raise questions about them which, as questions, have enormous significance; but unless we can make contact with a source of information which is outside the range of

human apprehension we cannot get answers on which
we can rely. For most of us the most important question to which we cannot know the answer is: Do we
cease to exist when we die? Only a being possessed of
higher powers of apprehension than us could know
the answer to that, and it would also have to be possible for us to have direct communication with him/it.
There are, I know, humans who believe that there are
such beings and that we do have such contact, and
that through them we know the answer to the question. This *could* be true. But it could also be true that
my living room is full of silent, invisible, intangible
monkeys. Both statements can easily be asserted, and
neither can be disproved. But there is no reason why
either should be taken seriously. People who believe
such things do so, I suspect, because they have a
powerful desire to. The wanting seduces them into
the deed without an intermediate process of considering seriously enough the relationship between answer and question.

I understand clearly what this problem is like because I have it myself with some of Schopenhauer's
metaphysics, though not all. Like every great philosopher, Schopenhauer made great mistakes, his two
greatest being about determinism and pessimism. But
away from his errors his philosophy is brimming with
good insights, some of them of unsurpassed depth.
They ring so true that for me they come close to
being compelling. I find myself *wanting* to believe
them—it would give me so much emotional and in-

tellectual satisfaction. And they could indeed be true. But what I can never get over is the fact that I have no way of knowing. That I am flooded with the feeling "Yes, surely this must be right" is not a validation, not even a credential. Total reality might be like that, but it might be nothing like that at all. How am I to know? The permanent unknowability of it gnaws at me. I could, of course, put an end to this by taking the plunge. But there could be no response more inappropriate and unjustified, however tempting.

It is natural for us to chafe against our ignorance in matters so fundamental and important. We long to know what cannot be known. In all societies there seem to have been people who cashed in on this by claiming to others, and possibly believing themselves, that they did know what could not be known—for instance, the future. Even in our unprecedentedly secular and rationalistic society, the most popular journals carry features that reveal to their readers what the future holds in store for them. Activities of this sort constitute the most familiar forms of charlatanry. The only one as common is the pretence to be able to cure. Both are perennial, because both give us illusions that we want so much to have that we are prepared to pay money, and sacrifice other things, to have them.

The resistance we feel against allowing the full extent of the unknown into our view of reality gives us a powerful drive to piece together a complete picture out of what we do know, or can know. But alas, the human situation is as if we were given some but not all of the pieces of a jigsaw puzzle and left to make a complete picture of them. Whatever we ended up with could not be the true picture. It would be possible, however, to have all the pieces in their right places and in their right relationships to one another if we renounced the aim of completeness, and tolerated gaps between the pieces. It is bound to yield more truth than forcing the pieces together, even though we have an almost irresistible urge to do so, and doing it might yield a picture that would look more coherent and meaningful, more suggestive, more satisfying.

So far, I have considered the operation on us of two causes of our permanent exclusion from the understanding of total reality: our location in time, and the limitations of the apparatus we have for understanding. The latter must, I take it, be the more fundamental. The former goes through a process of continuous rectification by the passage of time for successive members of the human race, whereas the latter will go on being the same for all of us, as long as we are human. From what proportion of total reality we are excluded we can never know, but we should assume it to be nearly all, because the amount of what is unknowable is illimitable, whereas what we know, and ever can know, is so little.

There exist lines of possibility that run counter to what I have been saying. One is that total reality is somehow rooted in us. A form of this is postulated by the philosophy of absolute idealism. Another is to be found in religions that postulate a creator god who has made everything, and has made human beings in his own image, so that we are partial sharers in the nature of whatever it is that has caused and created everything. In the first case the world is my creation. In the second my nature mirrors an aspect of whatever it is that has caused and created everything. Notoriously often it is impossible to prove a negative, and I cannot prove (nor can anyone else) that absolute idealism is false; but I find myself unable to believe that the totality of what there is depends on me for its existence. Similarly, I have never found myself able to believe in the existence of a god, though again I cannot prove his non-existence, just as no one can prove his existence. Belief is not under the control of the conscious will. It often happens that we would like to believe some things, and may even try to make ourselves do so, but find ourselves unable to. The beliefs of which I have just spoken are anthropomorphic. To extend my metaphysical understanding I am driven in other directions.

Since the discrediting of Marxism, few intellectually serious people have deluded themselves that they know what the future holds. Almost all of it is blank to us, yet thankfully fewer of us now than formerly treat this as a licence to believe what we like. In other areas we need the same spontaneous refusal to accept ignorance as a reason for belief. Bad method would have us believe in the truth of an explanation for no other reason than that we find ourselves unable to think of a better one: worse method accepts it because we would like it to be true. In all such cases an active agnosticism is required, agnosticism as a positive principle of procedure, an openness to the fact that we do not know, followed by intellectually honest enquiry in full receptivity of mind. Our ignorance stretches indefinitely beyond the bounds of what we know. And none of the significant bounds are set by language. Indeed, far from the limits of what is linguistically intelligible to us determining the limits of what we can apprehend, the truth is the opposite: the limits of what we can apprehend determine the limits of what is linguistically intelligible to us. Nor is it only at a frontier surrounding our total picture that unintelligibility begins. There are huge, indeterminate areas of unintelligibility within the picture itself, some of them at the centre of it.

These empty spaces at the heart of our understanding are as close to our consciousness as anything can be. They include consciousness itself, which I suspect is going to prove permanently unintelligible and inexplicable. There are also the operations of our will. All the time I am awake I am carrying out willed actions, yet how I do it is a mystery to me. I decide to pick up a teacup, so I pick it up. There is nothing easier, you could say: no problem there. But how do I do it? No amount of introspection enables me to perceive or grasp the process by which my will, or the decision I take, directs the movement of my hand. As

Chomsky once said to me (Bryan Magee, *Men of Ideas*, p. 214): "As soon as questions of will, or decisions, or reasons, or choice of action, arise, human science is pretty much at a loss.... These questions remain in the obscurity that has enveloped them since classical antiquity." Yet such experiences are at or near the centre of our conscious awareness a great deal of the time, and for that reason constitute a large part of our awareness of being alive. And then again there is ethics. When Wittgenstein says, "Ethics is transcendental," he has just, at that point, written: "It is clear that ethics cannot be put into words." He cannot mean by this that we are unable to say "This is right but that is wrong," because we do. What is more, we try to live by it. I think he must mean that what cannot be put into words is what our reasons are for saying it—and perhaps what it is we are saying when we do say it, despite the fact that we think we know what we mean.

Except for psychopathic paedophiles we all, I take it, have a conviction that torturing children for pleasure is wrong; but as individuals we give different reasons why it is wrong. Some of us think it is wrong because it offends God's law. Others do not believe there is a god, and think it wrong because they have compassion for the child. Yet others think it wrong because of the requirements of human beings living together successfully. Explanations different from any of these also have adherents. However, common to everybody is a strong feeling of certainty that the deed is wrong. It is something about which we are unwavering: we do not budge, we do not have the slightest doubt. Yet the disconcerting truth is that we do not *know* what the reasons for the wrongness are. Here is something we all "know" and are sure of, but we do not know *why*, in any serious sense of the word "know." It is obvious that being sure cannot be a guarantee of truth, still less the fact that many of us have reached the same conclusion by different routes. Perhaps our fundamental mistake is searching for reasons at all. Perhaps things are not right or wrong for reasons. In practice we shall go on upholding a shared certainty based on a chaos of incompatible "reasons." Only a handful of fanatics would consider it essential to achieve unity of belief before we can agree on action.

We are in a similar position with statements of aesthetic value, though the stakes are usually not so high. Nearly all music lovers are agreed that Mozart is a great composer and, what is more, a greater composer than Schumann. We are constantly saying things like this, but what it is that the words actually mean is something we find impossible to spell out, let alone agree on. In art neither greatness nor depth can be pinned down, but we find the concepts indispensable. We regard Shakespeare's *King Lear* and *Hamlet* as plays of incomparable depth, and indeed they are, but what does "depth" mean here? Can anyone tell us? We use such statements all the time, but a satisfactory justification for them, or even a clear explanation of what they mean, eludes us. We *think* we know what they mean, but we cannot express that meaning in any words other than the statements in which we make use of it. Attempts to do so result inevitably in controversial and incompatible formulations. Then there are other people who come along and, because we cannot provide satisfactory explanations, assert that the statements are invalid. It is illegitimate, they tell us, to say that Mozart is a great composer, and even more illegitimate to say that he is a greater composer than Schumann. And it is meaningless to say that *Hamlet* is a play of real depth. Of course all this is pure nonsense. It is an extreme example of people striving to exclude the un-understood from their view of what we know. Not only are value statements and ethical statements meaningful, their meanings express things that are at the very heart of life. They are necessary even to honesty, because if we say we are unable to assert whether torturing children for pleasure is wrong, or Mozart is a great composer, we are denying what we know to be true. Those who claim that such statements express no more than personal preferences are in a last-ditch-stand of desperation. To deny the statements any more legitimacy than that is not only to restrict our conception of reality to what we can provide good reasons for, it is also to confine our conception of what can be known to what can be satisfactorily expressed in language.

Experience leads me to suspect that among the causes why so many people deny that ethical statements and value statements can be true, and give as their reason the fact that such statements cannot be rationally validated, is a fear of letting religion in by the back door. It is a baseless fear. In any honest intellectual enquiry there is no place for religion. At best it is distorting, because from the moment it is introduced an assumption of its legitimacy has been made, and something about possible outcomes has been either pre-selected or precluded, and the balance of possibilities rigged. In hard reality the greater part of it is intellectually impoverished. And it is simply not the case that if we cannot now provide a rational explanation of something, we have no alternative but to accept a different sort of explanation from those currently available. There is, it is true, a tendency on our part to suppose that one or other of these is correct, so if this is not the right one, then another of them must be. But the plain fact is that often all the explanations on offer are wrong, and we are in a position of not knowing, not being able to explain the phenomenon in question until a new idea or discovery comes along. And meanwhile we must learn to live with our ignorance. Ignorance is a compelling reason for *not* believing, not for believing.

When religious people say to me, as they do: "Why won't you accept our calling the noumenal 'God'?" my reply is: "Because you have no grounds for doing so. To do that implies a characterisation of it, and insinuates an attitude towards it. You have no justification for the implying, or the insinuating, or the

characterisation. You are allowing yourself to think
you are in a position you are not in—and then pro-
ceeding from there." Religious discourse has this general characteristic. It is a form of unjustified evasion,
a failure to face up to the reality of ignorance as our
natural and inevitable starting-point. Anyone who
sets off in honest and serious pursuit of truth needs
to know that in doing that he is leaving religion behind. Unless he is prepared to do that, and to acknowl-
edge to himself that he has, he will not even have set
out on the journey—nor can he, because the position
he is in is not an honest and genuine starting-point.
Like a false premise in an argument, it will under-
mine the legitimacy of everything that follows.

THREE

The Human Predicament

WE HAD NO SAY IN EXISTING—WE WERE NOT GIVEN any choice. We just woke up into the world and found ourselves in it. Later, after we reach a certain age, opting out of it becomes a possibility, in the form of suicide—but only after the event, when we have started to live. By then most of us are in thrall to an instinct for survival that is programmed into us biologically. We are here now, and we want to go on living; so we try to make the best of it.

So we, who do not know what we are, have to fashion lives for ourselves in a universe of which we know little and understand less. One essential aspect of our situation is that we are social creatures, indeed social creations: each one of us is created by two other people. If we are not cared for by them, or someone taking their place, we die. Our existence and our survival both require active involvement by others. So we live out our lives on the surface of this planet in families, groups, societies, all of which have their own structures and rules, their own general modes of being and ways of behaving. These are already in place before we join them. They empower us in many ways, but they also partially shape us and partially limit us. We accommodate ourselves to them with varying combinations of success and failure. They are diverse and ephemeral in their forms, part of the ever-changing surface of life; but it is a crucial fact that none of them can alter the fundamental truths about the individual's being in the universe, which are everywhere the same. Whatever society we find ourselves in, wherever its location in space and time, we need to be procreated by other individuals, then born, then nurtured. And only then can we live what may or may not be a partially self-directed life in a "container" of space and time, alongside other persons and objects. Then we die. In all societies that is the basic pattern of human existence. No society can change it. Nor can any society do more than a limited amount to alter the physical bodies that we have, or are, with their intricate and variegated equipment. So by comparison with these universal, inescapable facts, the particular forms of the society in which we find ourselves have only secondary significance. This is why all explanations of human being that present themselves primarily in terms of social forms are miscast: the essentials of life are not subject to such differences. This is something the greatest minds (for instance, Shakespeare) always understood. It is why many explanatory theories such as, for instance, Marxism are shallow. I take Marxism as an instance because *Marxisant* attitudes still have influence in the arts, and are so attached to social differences that they have none but the thinnest cosmetic illumination to cast on art or life. Like other cosmetics they direct attention away from the substance of reality to its surface.

There is something altogether primal in the relationship of the individual to the universe which is absent from the relationship of the individual to society. He can choose to live in a different society, and millions do, but he cannot choose to live in a different universe. Perhaps for this reason we take the unchangeable relationship for granted most of the time. Our conscious concerns are mostly wrapped up in our relationships with other people, in whatever social world we inhabit.

As beings in the universe we are material objects. It is possible that we are more than that, and millions believe that we are, but there are other millions who believe we are not. The question is controversial. But one thing we have to agree on is that we are *at the very least* material objects. But then the extraordinary thing is that we are material objects that know

themselves from inside. This is an amazing fact—I
am tempted to say a mystical fact. Yet unless we are ill
or handicapped, or feeling our age, not much of our
inner activity of thought and feeling has the body
itself as its object. Most of the time our conscious
awareness is of people and things outside ourselves.
Even most of our thoughts about ourselves are not
about our bodies but about situations in which we
find ourselves, especially with regard to people and
work—and then, in those connections, with our wants
and projects, our responsibilities and anxieties, our
hopes and fears, immediate intentions. These are the
terms in which our "inner" lives are mostly lived.

So although it is an extraordinary and consequential truth that we know ourselves from inside, it is an
even more consequential truth that what we know is
largely not material. I am not directly aware of my
brain as a material object, nor of my skeleton, heart,
stomach, lungs, kidneys, intestines, and all the other
material things that go to make up me. Not even by
an act of will can I make myself aware of most of
them. Far from knowing them well, I do not know
some of them at all, and have little idea how they
function. I scarcely know where some of them are,
still less what they look like. I am fairly sure I would
be startled by the appearance of many of them, and
would find the sight of them alarming, if not disgust-
ing. A lot of people—children obviously, but many
adults too—have little idea of the organs that go to
make them up. In fact, the truth is that this is not what

human beings think of themselves as being. I have been living in or with my body for more than eight decades now, but it has never occurred to me to think of myself as *it*. I own it and am in it, as a driver owns and is in a car; and in the same way what happens to it can kill me or injure me. It exerts all sorts of influences on my life, from the important to the trivial. But I am not *it*. At least, I have never supposed or imagined that I am.

However, although I do not feel myself to be these organs, muscles, bones, etc.—even if, in aggregate, they constitute me—I do not feel myself to be my outside either. Yet this dominates the view of me that other people get. Sometimes, unexpectedly—usually while crossing a road—I find myself walking towards a full-length reflection of myself in a shop window without, for just a split second, realizing it is me. There, hunched and thrusting towards me, comes an old man in his eighties, big-built, white-haired, bespectacled. Only after this instant of perception do I realise it is me. And what a shock that is! That is not at all how I think of myself, nor is it how I feel myself to be. The truth is that none of us, unless he is an identical twin, knows what he looks like. In many years as a television broadcaster I was familiar with the astonishment expressed by people when they saw themselves on film or videotape for the first time: they simply had no idea they looked like that. The same thing was true with the sound of their voices. When they heard themselves on tape for the first time

it sounded to them like a voice they had never heard
before, the voice of a stranger. In the case of voices,
at least, there is a clear physical reason. We hear the
voices of others as transmitted through the air between their mouths and us, but we hear our own
voices only partly through the air, the rest through
vibrations inside our heads, including the bones of
our skull, so the physics of the sound is different.

The fact is, then, that although people know their
own bodies from within, they do not know them all
that well—neither from within nor from without. I
can see a bit of the front part of my outside, from the
chest downwards. But only indirectly, from reflections
and pictures, do I know what my face looks like. I
directly see the faces of other people all the time, but
never my own. I have often surmised that if I were to
find myself sitting in a railway compartment opposite
someone identical to myself, I would notice all sorts
of things about him that I am not normally aware of
about myself. For instance, although I know this in
the abstract, I suspect I would be taken aback to see
how big I am. And I know from the shop-window
experience that I would find the sight of myself in
action alien and startling, if not disturbing.

Some readers may think: "Naturally you do not
feel yourself to be your body's *parts*, and cannot make
yourself aware of most of them even if you try. But
you feel yourself to be your body as a whole. The
aggregate is you, a you that you are aware of being.
And you are aware of this from inside, not from out-

side. Every time you move, you are subliminally aware of your body as a whole. You are steering it, and positioning it at will, all the time you are awake. You are also aware of it in other ways: hunger and thirst, itches and pains, tiredness...." My response is to concede that all this is true, but to say that it leaves a lot out. If I look at another person I see his body as a whole, a head on a trunk with four limbs, but that is not how I feel myself to be. Actually, I do not see the other person as *being* that either. Just as the being in myself of which I am aware is mostly not that of my body, so the being of other people of which I am mostly aware is not that of their bodies. I do not see other people primarily as material objects. I do not look at another person in the way I look at an armchair or a rock. I see people, unlike things, primarily in terms of intangibles: their personalities and characters, their movements, responses, expressions (especially of feeling), gestures, behaviour, intentions, wishes and the like. In other words, my ways of apprehending other people overlap extensively with my ways of apprehending myself. There is a whole world—which they and I partially share and partially do not share—of thoughts, feelings, wants, aims, drives, memories, moods, and other such things. And it mostly is *such* things. Bodies come into it, but unless we are making love (and perhaps even then) they disappear into a larger picture. Furthermore, for most of the time when I am with other people I am more aware of them than I am of myself. I am even, usually, more aware of the material objects in front of me than I am of my own body. For much of my daily existence my sense of being is absorbed in an intense taking-in of my surroundings—so intense that it is almost as if I *am* my surroundings. Fichte expressed this in a superb phrase: "I am a living seeing." Kant argued that it would not be possible for us to be conscious of our own existence if we were not also conscious of things outside ourselves. Most of my awareness of being alive is an awareness of being-in-the-world, an ever-ongoing, *interactive* involvement with other people and things.

In a way reminiscent of Chomsky's contention that, contrary to what had always been assumed, our acquisition of a language cannot be explained satisfactorily by the linguistic input to which we are exposed as children, I contend that our knowledge and understanding of other people, and our relations with one another, cannot be explained by the observable exchanges we make with one another. Something else is going on as well. A particular and extreme—and for that reason clear-cut and useful—example of this is provided by orchestral conducting. Many music lovers are able to hear the difference between two recordings of the same work conducted by, shall we say, Toscanini and Sir Thomas Beecham, but no one seems able to explain how each of these is arrived at, ranging as they do from the unity of the overall architecture down to each individual detail and its integration into the whole. Such things cannot be fully

explained in terms of what the conductor says at re-
hearsals (which often is not much) plus the way he
looks at the musicians and waves his arms about. An
immense amount that we cannot account for is being
communicated by one person to dozens of others
who carry out his wishes in subtle detail. I have long
been fascinated by this, and have discussed it across
the years with orchestral players and conductors. Players agree immediately, and without question, that
they play differently for different conductors, but they
cannot account for why, still less for how the *what*
that is required of them is communicated to them.
Conductors know what they are doing, and can do it
at will, but they can no more explain *how* they do it
than I can explain how I move my fingers, though I
do that at will too. Here we have a highlighted example of something that, it seems to me, is going on
amongst us human beings all the time. It is impossible to account for the warm, capacious, deep, detailed, sophisticated and rich understanding that we
have of one another in terms of our attention to one
another's words plus our observation of one another's bodily movements. Something else, of a different
order, is going on. And like so much else that is everyday, we do not know how to account for it; but
this is not to say that it does not happen, still less that
it is occult or supernatural. It is that we do not yet
have an explanation for it. The conductor Bruno Wal-
ter used to assert that conducting was an occult activity, but I consider it a mistake to explain the not-yet-

understood in terms of the supernatural: it pre-empts
enquiry, and forestalls more accurate and informative
explanations.

In a context such as this it is always important to
remember that rational explanations have ongoing histories: they are invented, criticised, argued for, argued
against, revised, reconstructed, salvaged, abandoned,
replaced, in a never-ending process. Just as innumerable things that are reasonably well understood now
were not understood until recently, so it has to be expected that all sorts of things that we do not understand now will be satisfactorily explained in the future. This is the natural order of events. But there are
many people who do not seem to realise it. If a natural explanation of something is not available now,
they assume it must have a supernatural explanation.
Such a to-us everyday phenomenon as electricity has
been understood for only about 200 years, and before
then occult, even religious explanations were widely
entertained. In the same way 200 years from now
whole worlds of accurate explanation will be available
concerning matters that are a closed book to us now,
or about which we have actively mistaken ideas. The
whole history of understanding consists of advances
of this kind. With regard to each thing we are trying
to understand we need to think about what stage we
are likely to be at in the history of its explanation.
There is something primitive in human nature that
works against this, and wants to reach out for the

reassurance of a supernatural, occult or religious explanation of the unknown. But, like so many primitive reactions, it is not a good way to go about things. It does more to prevent understanding than to increase it.

This applies to all the mysteries of human intercommunication—for instance, the expressivity of our eyes. According to the laws of physics, we see the eyes of other people because the light in the air around them is reflected to us from the surface of their eyeballs. Nothing is directed outwards from inside the eye itself—no light rays, and nothing else that any of the sciences can tell us about. Yet eyes can be more subtly expressive than language in our communication with one another. They are especially revealing of our inner states. Our deep selves are in communication through our eyes. We know this to be a fact, even though present-day science has nothing to offer us by way of an explanation. It is far more probable that there will one day be a natural explanation of it than that the true explanation is supernatural.

But we need neither eyes nor tongues to communicate with one another's inner selves. The physical presence of another human being, whom we do not see and who does not say anything, can be comforting, even life-saving. Such a person is not just another material object in the space outside us. It is as if there is what one might call a metaphysical space which that person shares with us—even as if, jointly, we *are* that metaphysical space. It is as if we are interconnecting parts of something. The feeling is palpable, and has vivid immediacy.

We do not even need to be in physical proximity for it to occur. If I say something on the telephone and it causes a sudden, unexpected silence at the other end, the inner response of that person is very often apparent to me in an instant. I know at once whether he is taken pleasantly by surprise or taken unpleasantly by surprise. I know if he is disappointed, or embarrassed, or shocked, or is merely savouring the newness of the thought I have just put to him. Or I know that he is pausing to consider the substance of his reply—or, quite differently, that he is about to say something non-committal and wants to choose his words carefully for that reason. There are innumerable possibilities of difference between the silent messages that convey themselves from him to me. But there are not different kinds of silence that convey them. Silence is silence. There is no sound at all. Yet the messages *are* conveyed. This cannot be explained in terms of my expectations, knowing from experience what sort of reaction the other person is likely to have, because quite often the reaction takes me by surprise and is not at all what I expected.

We grow up in multiple forms of contact with one another that carry on all the time, consisting mostly of invisible connections—wants and their expression, their satisfaction or frustration; affection and the desire for it, or fear of losing it; beliefs, assumptions, ex-

pectations, co-operation and competition, demands
on us and prohibitions, rules; respect, admiration,
dislike; and a thousand other things, in the totality
of which not only our modes of visible and aural
communication but also our modes of inner communication have their living roots. The sense of contact
we are able to have with someone to whom we are
close goes a long way beyond anything language can
cope with, and is enigmatic to us. (There is evidence,
incidentally, that the word "enigma" in the title of
Elgar's *Enigma Variations* refers not to a hidden musical theme but to friendship.) At its most intense, in
love, it is held by many to be the most valuable thing
in life, the highest of all values. Some even say that
God is love.

So at some level underneath what presents itself to
our senses and our conscious minds we are in direct
communication with one another, and the inner
being of each one of us is involved. This might help
to explain why most of us find it so hard to live alone.
Connection with another human being is not a mere
top-up to our separate existence, an optional extra.
Although it is rare for humans to experience long
periods of solitary isolation, when they do they quite
often either go mad or commit suicide. It seems literally impossible for a solitary piece of humanity to remain alive and uncracked for many years. Our need
for communication goes as deep as our being—which
is itself a mysterious creation of other people, so that
the very seed-germ of our being emerges from an act

of intercommunication. I take it that the intensest
form of intercommunication is love. It is significant
that we talk of love being "consummated" in the act
of love, as if it cannot remain within one person and
be fully itself. Perhaps there is a parallel here with the
creative artist, who does not just feel a need to create
a work of art and then, separately from that, a need to
communicate it to others: for him the act of communication is intricately involved with the work itself,
and is also part of the creative process. Intercommunication is at the heart of human existence.

It seems to me probable that morality is rooted in
the sense of immediate contact that we have with one
another's inner selves. It is as if we share the same
inner being, though to say this is to hurl an idea a long
way out in front of our present knowledge. However,
it does fit our experience uncannily and comprehen-
sively. Be that as it may, we must at the very least be
profoundly similar in our inner being to experience
the kinds of contact with one another that we do,
and to make possible such things as self-identification
with others, and accurate mutual anticipation, and
compassion. The existence of these modes of contact
provides us with the best general rules we have for
understanding one another. We will usually get our
predictions about others approximately right if we
ask ourselves: "How would I feel in his situation?" It
is this question that gives us also the cornerstone of
our morality, the so-called Golden Rule, common to
nearly all the classic systems of ethics, including the

main religious ones: "Treat others as you would wish yourself to be treated." In fact, the notion of inner oneness may possibly contain the key not only to morality but to the enigma of life itself. According to the theory of evolution, a living individual existence has been passed on unbrokenly, continuous, self-renewing, from the amoeba to everyone living today.

The fact that all these possibilities imbue our lives without our fully understanding them induces a sense of wonderment. We are awestricken by our situation. We are so small in every way compared with what there is, and so ignorant. Mystery surrounds us on every side. And our destiny is not in our own hands. Some of the things for which we have no explanation are of the utmost importance to us, above all life itself—and then, within life, consciousness and love, and the highest of the moral considerations, then sex, music, and the rest of the arts; all marvellous and all inexplicable. Individual works of art may speak to us in ways whose meaningfulness engulfs us, yet what they express is inexpressible in any other terms. I would take the mysteriousness of all this to be self-evident were it not for the fact that so many deny it. As for human existence, we know that it is only a tiny part of the whole of existence, yet few of us seem to think beyond it. I suspect that our own little world, the world of Nature on this planet, is the outer limit for most of us. That could be why so many believe that we human beings have emerged from Nature by processes which science can, in principle, explain fully—so that even if our explanations are not complete yet, they are on course to become so. This point of view is deeply uncomprehending. Several of the greatest philosophers, in different centuries—Locke, Kant and Wittgenstein, for instance, differing among themselves though they do—have explained to us how the world of experience, the world of Nature, the world investigated by science, is a field of interaction between two inexplicables, these being experiencing subjects and things as they are in themselves. From this it would follow that the experiencing subject cannot be wholly within the world of its own experience, and also that things as they are in themselves cannot be wholly within that world either. So we humans are partially in this world and partially not. Many have believed that the interface between the two must be where the key to the ultimate mystery of our existence lies.

The fact that the self is not to be found in Nature may explain, or may help to explain, the widely held conviction (which I share) that a self is not an object or a thing, and therefore cannot justifiably be treated as such. It should not, except as the lesser of two evils, be destroyed or damaged. It has its significance partly outside this world, and its value (like that of morals and the arts) is a not-entirely-of-this-world value. I refrain from quoting other philosophers too often in this book, but on this point I cannot resist recalling Wittgenstein's blunt: "The subject does not belong to the world: rather, it is a limit of the world."

Later in the *Tractatus* he says: "If there is any value which does have value, it must lie outside the whole sphere of what happens and is the case.... It must lie outside the world." We cognise these truths as we cognise the existence and identity of other people: we *do* it, and cannot be in any doubt that we do it, but we do not altogether understand how we do it, still less what it is we are doing.

In the case of morality the form of cognition is a peculiar one which consists not only in recognizing certain propositions to be true but also in acknowledging that their truth needs to influence our behaviour. If it is indeed the case that morality is rooted in some sort of sharedness of inner being, that would explain why we are so immediately aware of moral imperatives in our relationship with others, and also why we are unable to support these imperatives conclusively with rational argument: they are not rooted in reason. And if it is logically impossible to provide morality with foundations of rational argument this cannot be a requirement of rationality. In that case it is no criticism of any given view of morality to say that it does not have rational foundations. If it did, it would be mistaken. The valid demands of rationality in that case are to account for why this is so, and to hold our moral convictions as being open to criticism at *that* level, a meta-level, where we are able to offer rational argument in response to disagreement. For instance, if you are in government and feel morally obliged to pursue a policy that minimises the loss of

innocent lives, you may be unable to support this with
rational arguments that carry conviction with religious and political fundamentalists, but you should
nevertheless be prepared to provide them with all the
rational arguments you can. If they resort to violence
you may then be justified, having used and exhausted
the resources of rational argument, in using violence
to stop them getting their way by violence.

Two things I am sure of are that morality does not
have as its basis either group opinion or social self-
interest. It cannot be *only* a social construct, though it
may be partially so. The fact that everyone has agreed
on something could never make the something morally right, nor could the fact that it is in everyone's
self-interest. A trivial example will suffice. If a group
of friends is about to go to a restaurant for dinner and
at the last moment someone who is not one of the
group but would like to become so tags along—and
then, when the bill comes, wants to pay it, because he
wants to ingratiate himself with the others—it is in
the self-interest of everyone present for him to pay.
But it is wrong for the others to let him. The fact that
it is wrong is independent of anyone's wishes, and
goes against everyone's self-interest. This tiny illustration reveals a major truth about ethics. It contains
an element of objectivity that renders it never wholly
explicable in terms of social considerations.

In some respects our aesthetic judgements are a
similar case. They may likewise be the subject of
convictions of great power and immediacy which are

based not on rationality but on direct experience, so that although we are able to some extent to support them with arguments, we are never able to do so conclusively. About these too we should be willing to listen to argument from others, and reply rationally to criticism. Although conclusive justification is not possible, worthwhile criticism is, and often helps to bring about an improvement in understanding. Here, as elsewhere, we are seeking not proof but progress, for here, as elsewhere, progress is possible but proof is not.

There exist some moral situations in which the right choice defies all rational defence. In one of Dostoevsky's novels a character says that if the prosperity and happiness of all future mankind could be secured by the torturing to death of a single child, and it were done, he would dissociate himself from humanity. I fear that in the real world his priorities would not be observed, but he is right. When I was a Member of Parliament I opposed torture being used against Irish terrorists to force them to give information that could save innocent lives, and I would do it again, but I found my position impossible to justify to the relatives of some of the innocent people who had been murdered by terrorists.

Whenever, like this, I have held to a moral conviction against rational considerations, the conviction has always been a negative one: I have felt that a certain course of action was wrong. I have never, with the same degree of conviction, thought I knew what was right. A linguistic philosopher would have no difficulty in formulating a positive proposition based on what I have just said whose truth I would have to say I felt sure about. But the difference of substance is fundamental, and is another instance of the fact that we can never be sure that something is right though we can be sure that something is wrong. Socrates used to say that he had an inner voice which occasionally told him not to do things, but it never told him what to do. I suspect there may be such a voice in most of us, obscured by the hurly-burly and welter that is our normal inner life, and speaking to us only occasionally.

Mention of Socrates recalls that there can be situations in which the greatest commitment of all occurs, an unconditional commitment transcending all considerations of life and death for the person making it. Socrates embraced death rather than do what he thought was wrong; furthermore, he did not get out of this situation when he could have done. In tragic plays and operas a hero in this position is a familiar figure, someone who sets his life at nothing by sticking to his course at the cost of his life, and refuses a proffered way out. When Martin Luther volunteered to make an appearance at the Diet of Worms that was likely to lead to his death, his entire speech is said to have been: "Here I stand. I cannot do otherwise. God help me." In situations like this the individual feels a sense of commitment that is his all in all, more important than life itself. Most of us would back down in such circumstances, giving to ourselves an excuse for a face-saving formula, as Galileo did under the Inquisition. Indeed, there are people hostile to unconditional self-dedication. They see it as unrealistic, and explain it either as fanaticism or as a form of narcissism in which the person puts his self-image above all other considerations—*he* must maintain *his* integrity, no matter what the cost. Or they see it as an over-the-top form of self-seeking in which, say, a person pursues martyrdom and sainthood. All these forms of behaviour do exist, but they need to be distinguished from the one I am describing. Socrates did more than any other individual in the history of Western civilisation to encourage radical self-questioning, which is the opposite of fanaticism. And although he was guilty of false modesty he does not seem to have been primarily concerned with his image. Being, as he was, surpassingly rational he seems to have seen ultimate moral sanctions as transcending both self and rationality.

There will be some readers who say to me: "You put forward two sets of arguments which, taken together, point to a third, yet you stop short of drawing the third as the obvious inference. First, you say it is almost certain that most of reality is unknown to us, and bound to remain so. Second, you say that, from within the world as we do know it, it is impossible to give a satisfactory account of, as you put it, 'everything that is most important to us—the nature of our inner selves, and also of other people's inner selves, and whether these selves have any lasting future; the nature of the world outside ourselves, the nature of time, the nature of space, the nature of objects in the world, our moral convictions; our responses to great art....' This suggests, obviously, that the real explanations of these things have their roots in that part of reality that is unknown to us. And you yourself say so. But is this not what adherents of the world's major religions have been saying all along? On this fundamental point, surely, they are right? Why are you so determined to keep them out of the discussion?"

I keep them out of the discussion because they use the very fact of our ignorance as the basis for their claim to be in possession of the truth. From facts such as that life and consciousness are incomprehensible, and that values in art and morals are rooted outside the empirical world, it does not follow that I and my readers have immortal souls, or that there is a God who created the world. These things are not connected logically. When religious people are forced to admit this they say: "God moves in a mysterious way." What kind of explanation is that? As Wittgenstein said, if the existence of the world we know is so miraculous that we feel a need to posit the existence of God to explain it, then the existence of God is even more miraculous, and how do we explain that? If one presses religious people for real explanations, explanations that really do explain, they retreat into protestations of how mysterious everything is, how far beyond human understanding. But we know that already. That is where we ourselves are coming from. What they are doing is using the ignorance we all share as a reason, so-called, for making unconnected assertions for which they can provide no foundations. And the worst of it is that these so-called explanations would not explain even if they were true, but would leave us shrouded in an even bigger mystery than before.

Reason can accomplish a great deal more than it yet has, and I feel confident that it will. The magnitude of its future advances is likely to dwarf those of the past, because the past of critical reflective thought is so short, whereas its future is indefinitely long. It would be in danger of being obstructed, contaminated, diverted, or even brought to a halt if we accepted religious intervention. The merest spoonful of religion in philosophy acts like a spoonful of sugar in coffee: it takes away the edge and insinuates blandness into the whole.

There are so many ways in which religious approaches are mistaken. First, existence simply could be arbitrary: everything that exists might just *be*, without there being an explanation. It seems to me that this has to be the case with the totality of everything there is, whether or not that includes a creator God. "How come everything (including God) exists?" looks to me like a question to which nothing could possibly be an answer. There is nothing else to which everything could be related, nothing else in terms of which it could be explained. At that level there might be no

"*Why?*" From the fact that a sufficient explanation of everything is not to be found within the world of our experience it does not follow that one must be found outside it. There may be no such explanation. Schopenhauer believed that. And it was for this, seen as the ultimate reality, that humanist existentialists employed the term "the absurd." Such people could be wrong. But they could be right. And a religious approach precludes the possibility.

Another way in which a religious approach is likely to be mistaken is in failing to take full account of the fact that explanations have developing histories. These perpetually alter the shape of the unknown. This connects up with the more general objection that it inevitably assumes too much. Even the most liberal, flexible and tentative assumes itself to be looking in the right direction when there is no reason to think that. All religion is an evasion, or partial evasion, of the mystery we confront. The unknown is unknown. Preconceptions about it, of any kind, corrupt and frustrate attempts to penetrate it.

The unknowable and unconceptualizable spill over into our empirical world. We live in amongst them all the time. We are mysteries to ourselves, and to one another. In our sexual relationships the miraculous happens, and happens again in the creation of new life. We do not understand life *or* death. Nor do we understand time. We are awestricken by the beauties of the world. When we listen to great music we glimpse unrealizable insights into the inner nature of reality.

The noumenal does not lie only on the outside of an empirical globe that contains all possible experience: it imbues experience itself, here, now, all the time. We ourselves are it—we ourselves are in some un-understandable way noumenal. In answer to the question "What is it about our empirical world that convinces you that there must be something else?" I am tempted to say "Everything." The world itself, as it is, its very existence, brims over with intimations of other realities and other orders of being. The challenge is to live in it (and die in it) without understanding it, and without closing our eyes to the fact that, whether we like this or not, it is our situation—and to do that without either, on the one hand, denying the mysteriousness of it or, on the other, grasping at supernatural explanations.

FOUR

Can Experience Be Understood?

THE CONCEPTION WE HAVE OF ANY INDIVIDUAL WE know nearly always starts with what he or she looks like. With most of our acquaintances this visual image always retains its lead—the instant their name is mentioned a visual image leaps into our minds. But this image is not any part of that person's being, it exists only in the eyes and minds of observers. It is not a constituent part of the body observed. Most of us have difficulty in envisaging what we look like to other people, precisely because our appearance is neither a part of our being nor a part of any experience we directly have ourselves. This is typical of the disjunction between things as we perceive them to be and those things as they are in themselves. It holds across the whole range of experience. And because the representations of perception and conception have no part in the being of their objects, the selfsame objects may be, and often are, apprehended in different ways by different people.

It is possible for a congenitally blind person to know another individual intimately, more intimately than most other people know that person, without there being any visual-image content. Our congenitally blind friends do not know what we or they look like, and have no solid conception of what it means to say that anybody looks like anything, yet their being is in other respects the same as ours. They look like the people they cannot see or form any visual conception of. But "look like" is a category to which nothing in their direct experience corresponds. Used literally, it can have content and significance only in relation to seeing, but for almost the whole of its history our universe has had no sighted creatures. Presumably, for much of that time, it was similar to what it is now—but what did it look like? Either we cannot allow any meaning to that question or we have to say that it "looked" as it does now.

The corresponding truth holds not only for each one of our senses but for each of our mental faculties. Our conceptions and apprehensions of things are not constituent parts of the things apprehended. Their only "reality" is as experiences: as experiences they are indeed real, but their existence is wholly dependent on our existence. It is not an independent existence.

There is an independently existing reality apart from us, but they are not it. They are a set of correlatives to our capacities. Things *as we apprehend them* are, and have to be, in the forms of our sensibilities, and in the categories of our understanding. We are in the sort of situation an airline pilot is in, who from moment to moment is basing everything he does on the reading and interpretation of gauges that give him detailed information about specific states of affairs which he is directly up against and which are very real indeed, of vital importance to him, but are totally different from gauges.

If you say to me: "All right, then: if this woman whom you have known intimately and loved for many years is not made up of the perceptions you have of her, who or what is she?" the only truthful answer I can give you is: "I don't know." Is she an immortal soul? I don't know. Is she a perishable mind attached to a perishable body? I don't know. Is she nothing more than a material object? I don't know. I do not know these things even about myself, let alone her. Not having any idea what the true nature is of things we know intimately is our normal situation, and applies to our entire knowledge of the world of objects, including people, including ourselves.

In some ways this is the most difficult thing of all for us to grasp. Even if we truly understand that our apprehensions of things have to be in forms provided by the equipment we have for apprehending, we can scarcely help envisaging their independent existence as corresponding to our perceptions of them. Our first response to the challenge this presents could be to react along the following lines—and let us, to begin with, think of a perceived object less complicated than a human being. You might say to me: "I can form a conception of that chair over there only in terms of its observational characteristics—its space-occupancy, what it looks like from every point of view, what it feels like to sit on, bump into, pick up, pat; the sounds it makes when I brush up against it or sink into it; all this plus everything revealed by a closer investigation, including measurements and a scientific analysis of the materials of which it is constructed. You cannot expect me to believe that each one of these characteristics is separate and free-floating, and that they all just happen by accident to have come together to give me the illusion of an object. There must be something there in which they inhere, so that none of them would be as they are if it were not as it is—so that what I am registering are *its* construction, *its* dimensions and weight, *its* materials and colours, *its* surfaces and textures; and these are providing me with my total picture of the chair. In this way, surely, my picture *corresponds* to the chair. So I see no reason why the chair should not be as I see it as being—and as I think of it as being when I am away from it. Why should objects *not* be as we apprehend and experience them, and as we think of them? What other way could there be for them to be?"

This response breaks down under interrogation. On analysis it turns out that no intelligible sense can be attached to words such as "like" or "as" in this context. A thing can be like another thing only if the two are of a more generally similar kind. There is no literal sense in which a colour can be like something that is categorially different from a colour: a colour can only be like, or not like, another colour. Visual data of any kind can only be like other visual data. A photograph can be like a landscape, but only in so far as both are visual data. If it is claimed that what the two have in common is something to do with their form (what the young Wittgenstein called their logical form) and that this is an abstraction, it is an abstraction that is intelligible only in relation to visual data, and is characteristic only of such data. It can no more exist independently of such data than a man's build can exist independently of his body. The same is true of everything that is yielded to our consciousness by our other senses, and also by our mental activities: a concept can be like only another concept. Basically, what is wrong with the objection we are considering is that it asks us to believe that sensory data *as such* can be like something categorially different from sensory data—not only "like" but "a copy"—and similarly that conceptions can be "like" something categorially different from conceptions. The mistake is easy to slip into—in fact it is difficult not to slip into it—because although we can query the categories of understanding that we have, we find ourselves unable to provide rationally defensible replacements for them.

When we live in the world of material objects in a
way that comes naturally to us, what we are doing is
reifying the contents of consciousness, taking them
to be independent entities that are apprehended by
us. In doing so we are attributing a separate existence to us-dependent phenomena. What we think
of as a chair is the aggregate of its us-dependent
characteristics—and we cannot help doing that, because there is no other way in which we could entertain any conception of it. Thus an illusion, or an almost irresistible tendency towards an illusion—what
might appropriately be called the illusion of realism—
is built into the human condition, and is an inher-
ent part of the logic of our situation. To think at all,
we have to think in terms of it, at least for most of
the time. It is almost impossibly difficult for us to
free ourselves from it. To do so by purely intellectual
means, which is the only solidly grounded way of
doing so,* requires not only self-discipline but an
unprecedentedly large-scale act of truly liberated intellectual imagination, including something like a
Gestalt-shift. It involves grasping that all our ways of
thinking, perceiving and experiencing are contingent
in their entirety; their very existence is not logically
necessary, because everything that exists apart from
us, whatever its nature, exists without them. Not

---

* There are religions whose metaphysical implications have something
in common with what I am saying, and which train some of their followers in meditation aimed at releasing them from the illusion of realism;
but such self-conditioning without an assured grasp of the intellectual
foundations of what is involved seems to me undesirable.

only is there no need for perceptions and concepts: until recently in the history of the universe there were no such things, and it is simply a fact that, apart from living beings, most of what exists exists without any relation to them. Reality is not, and cannot be, "like" representations or thoughts.

This realisation is disturbing. We have a profound need, rooted in our need for survival, to believe that what exists does so in terms we can understand. The recognition that this is not so, and cannot be so, is disorienting. For these as well as other reasons we may not find it practically possible to let go of the idea that reality has the character of our experience. Most people, it would seem, never give that up, including most philosophers. They spend their lives in thrall to the self-contradictory assumption that epistemological objects, objects as we apprehend them in experience, exist independently of experience.

Because to think "outside" that assumption requires not so much intelligence as a radically free yet prehensile act of intellectual imagination, misunderstanders include individuals of the highest intelligence. The form of imagination required is rarer than intelligence. The most gifted of creative artists have it, including great writers, but I fear not many academics.

If it is true that independent reality transcends any possible experience we could have of it, this has profound implications for our understanding of death. For with death we cease to inhabit the empirical world, and the empirical world ceases to inhabit us. But if

the empirical world is not independent reality, the relationship we have with independent reality may not
be at an end. There have always been many religious
people who believed this—who believed that for the
duration of our lives in the empirical world we are
exiles from the world of *real* reality, with which we
are reunited when we die. There may be some truth
in this or there may not. I do not know. But it is a
possibility. However, there is another apparent possibility that runs parallel to it but is apparent only, not
a genuine possibility—and yet a large number of people take it to be.

All actual experience is for a subject, a sentient
being who has the experience. With my death the
experiences in this world of one sentient being will
come to an end. Also, with the destruction of my
body I shall cease to exist as an object in the multiple
but separately unique worlds of other people. In the
same way, with the death of every other individual,
another unique sequence of experiences will come to
an end, and he too will soon cease to exist as an empirical object in the worlds of others. What cannot
happen, however, since there is no possible way in
which it could, is the continuance of an empirical
world without anyone in it at all—or perhaps I should
say, without any minds in it. A world that exists only
in experience could not exist if there is no experience.
Yet this seems to be what most of us unthinkingly
assume. We suppose that with the death of all of us,
the world as we know it would carry on without us.

Kant is clear about the impossibility of this, in a statement that rules out the commonest of all misunderstandings of his work. "If the subject, or even only the subjective constitution of the senses in general, be removed ... all the relations of objects in space and time, nay, space and time themselves, would vanish. As appearances, they cannot exist in themselves, but only in us. What objects may be in themselves, and apart from all this receptivity of our sensibility, remains completely unknown to us. We know nothing but our mode of perceiving them—a mode which is peculiar to us, and not necessarily shared in by every being, though, certainly, by every human being."

Anyone who protests "but of course the empirical world could go on existing without us in it" has radically failed to understand what is being said. He is not bound to *agree* with what is being said, but it represents a coherent and formidable view of such immense intellectual power that there cannot be any "of course" about its denial—if it is wrong, it is not wrong "of course." "Of course" people reveal in those very words that they have no conception of the act of intellectual imagination that is required for an understanding of this viewpoint. If all experiencing subjects one day cease to exist, whatever is not experience will go on existing, but by definition that cannot be an empirical world.

In not being able to form any conception of "what it will be like" after we die our situation has something in common with our not being able to conceptualise what it is like now. We cannot form any conception of the multitudinous empirical worlds that exist now, apart from our own. We know that billions of separate consciousnesses are at this very moment aware of a world, and we know that each of them is different from every other, but the sum of the unique experiences thus occurring simultaneously is not something that can be present in a single consciousness, at least not in this world. Schrödinger wrote that consciousness is a singular of which the plural is unknown, but I find myself reflecting that he should have added "and unknowable, though we know it to exist. *Knowing* it is a form of consciousness attributed to God."

When I die this unique empirical world of my knowledge and experience (and memories) will come to an end. What happens then will depend on the relationship, if there is one, between, on the one hand, me and my empirical world *taken together*, reciprocal as they are, and on the other hand whatever exists independently of them. It could be that I and my empirical world relapse into nothingness. But this is not certain. What presents itself to me now as nothingness might be as deceptive in this as the empty air around me before I switch on my pocket radio, or the visual world to a congenitally blind man about to get his sight. I am not confident about this—in fact, I am exceedingly doubtful—but the possibility exists.

FIVE

Where Such Ideas Come From

IN THIS BOOK MY AIM IS TO EXPRESS MY THOUGHTS AS directly as I can on the fundamentals of the human situation. These thoughts arose mainly in response to living, indeed as an essential part of living. I have, it is true, searched extensively for help in the writings of others, especially during long periods when I felt beleaguered. And what is more, I found it. Several writers fed important tributaries into my outlook, helped me, expanded my insights, rescued me from errors. However, my first concern was always with my own existential situation, not with what others have written; I was always trying to make sense of my own

understanding, not that of others. I am intensely interested in what others have thought only in so far as
it helps me and is grist to my mill. Because of that I
quote a few, but not many, of the philosophers I have
learnt from, though I do take advantage of the vo-
cabulary they developed for the discussion of ideas.

The considerations that led me to my basic position started from personal experience in the most literal sense, bodily experience. Two realisations influenced me in particular. First, that it is a contingent
truth, not a necessary one, that we have the bodily
equipment we have, including our sense organs, our
brains, and our central nervous systems, all of which
are tangible things, material objects, bits of stuff. This
equipment could have been other than it is: there
exist sentient creatures with sensory equipment different from ours. It is not only that there are moths that
can smell a potential mate a mile away, and lynxes
and hawks that can see detail at distances impossible
for the human eye: there are creatures who have different senses from ours altogether. Bats are equipped
with something like sonar, and perceive objects in a
way that works on the same principle as radar. Imag-
inably, we too could have been equipped with something like that—and with an indefinite number of
other alien senses. To the responsiveness we already
have to light rays could have been added the rays
of radio, television, infra-red and X-ray. There are
unknowable other possibilities that we cannot now
conceptualise, any more than humans could, until re-

cently, have conceptualised those I have mentioned. If we had many of them, our apprehension of the reality around us would be unimaginably different from what it is. As things are, we have the five fundamental senses we have: sight, hearing, touch, smell and taste; and we have our brains and central nervous systems to transform, store and make use of the information those senses give us. It is worth reiterating that this is physical equipment, all of it, not anything abstract: it consists of chunks of matter, material organs that function in particular ways and not in other ways.

We are able to supplement their physical operations in two main respects. Firstly, we invent devices to expand their range. There are a large number of these. In the case of seeing we provide ourselves with spectacles for daily use, and telescopes and microscopes to enable us to see things that are more distant, or smaller, than eyes with spectacles can see. In the case of thinking we provide ourselves with computers that perform in a very short time calculations that would take our brains a very long time, perhaps longer than a lifetime. Secondly, we have devices to pick up and translate for us signals that our personal equipment cannot register at all—I have instanced infra-red rays, X-rays, radio waves and television waves. In all such cases we have to include in our devices pieces of apparatus like dials, gauges and print-outs that translate their findings into a form that is intelligible to the bodily apparatus we do have. Our man-made devices, to be of use to us, must eventually deliver their output in a form that our built-in personal apparatus can make contact with and understand. There has, in the end, to be something we can see, feel, hear, taste or smell, and something our minds can get hold of. Otherwise nothing gets through to us.

This was the earliest of the considerations that led me to think that there must be a limit to what it will ever be possible for us to know. The second was the realisation that the forms of our sensibility and the categories of our understanding could not be what they are independently of the bodily apparatus whose modes of operation they are. A concept is something in a mind, so if there were no minds, there could be no concepts. For humans there could no more be thoughts without brains than there could be digestion without stomachs and intestines. We may have created machines that do our digesting for us, or our calculations, but it is we who invent and build the machines, and we do it to meet our needs and serve our purposes. We build our purposes into our machines, whose functioning and output are such as to be intelligible to our senses and minds. No machine would be able to give us visual data if we had no eyes, or aural data if we had no hearing. Nothing could intelligibly be said to be tangible if there were no such thing as touch. All the forms and categories in terms of which we perceive or conceive anything at all, with the aid of no matter what technologies or theories, are dependent for their ultimate intelligibility on the nature of our bodily apparatus, which is contingent.

In fact that too has evolved as it has in order to serve our purposes.

From these premises conclusions of the first magnitude follow. We are permanently able to form a conception of anything at all only in forms and categories that are available to us. We can understand only in the modes of understanding that we have, and these are both contingent and drastically limited. The very words "conception" and "understanding" refer to entities that are mind-dependent. So far as we know, until the merest flicker of time ago in what we take to be the history of the universe there were no such things as minds. And these exist, as far as we know, only on this planet. So although the standard measure of distance in the universe is the light-year, and most of its bodies are millions of light-years apart, if the theory of evolution is even roughly on the right lines the only bodily and mental apparatus capable of understanding anything at all has been developed recently, and for the specific purpose of living organisms' survival on or near the crust of this one particular planet. We cannot get outside our apparatus. In fact, in one sense, we *are* our apparatus.

I am not, it has to be understood, saying that we conceive things or states of affairs as being mind-dependent. Not at all. It is concepts themselves, not what they are concepts *of*, that are mind-dependent. Some critics of the view I am putting forward take me to be confusing the two, but it is they who are confusing the two. We can and do conceive things as existing independently of ourselves and our minds. Most of our conceptions, most of the time, are of things as existing independently of ourselves and our minds. But the existence of conceptions themselves can not possibly be independent of us. Concepts are inescapably in minds, or are derived from minds, even though what they are concepts of is usually not in minds. And the existence of concepts, their very nature and their functioning, are subject to the limitations that dependence on minds carries with it.

The concept "time" is not time, any more than the concept "a table" is a table. Investigations into the empirical world are not the same as investigations into concepts, although for a hundred years philosophy suffered from a high level of confusion between the two. I have always emphasised that reality—by which I mean what exists and is the case—is whatever it is regardless of us and our concepts, and therefore regardless of language. But I have also stressed that the concepts of reality that we humans form are inescapably mind-dependent. A concept can be only of something that it is possible for a concept to be a concept of, and with regard to specific empirical reality this excludes what lies outside the possibility of experience (if experience is taken to include also what can be inferred or imagined on the basis of experience). For instance, we cannot conceptualise a new primary colour. We can clearly and meaningfully think that there might be new (to us) primary colours somewhere, but we cannot conceptualise any such actual colour. The significant having of empirical concepts is always subject to the limitation of experiences. And since our worldview could not be as it is independently of our human apparatus, and since the universe existed in time for aeons before there were any minds, and since the universe stretches immeasurably beyond our knowledge in space as well as in time, it is as certain as anything can be that unimaginably vast amounts of reality exist which our apparatus can not mediate. What exists independently of us cannot—in itself, independently of being apprehended by us—exist in the forms that our faculties and our experience, including our imaginations, yield to us, because all of these are us-dependent. *In itself*, reality's mode of existence must be unintelligible to us. This is so with regard even to our own existence.

The fact that we can derive our conception of everything only through the resources we have, and through them alone, means that we do. We have no choice. Only in terms of the means at our disposal can we understand anything at all. We acquire a world-picture that exists entirely in terms of what can be seen, heard, felt, tasted and smelt; plus what can be thought, inferred, remembered, recorded, postulated, conjectured, intuited, invented, calculated and the rest; plus what can be put together out of these things, and what can be imagined from them, as if reality itself were like what our apparatus is capable of doing. Our whole conception of things, of everything, is made up in the end of what our equipment can deliver or conjecture, and therefore, primarily, of mental and sensory data, real and imagined. Because we can envisage only what is envisageable, and the envisageable is the limit of what can be envisaged, it seems self-evident to us that the envisageable is all there is, and all there could possibly be, because nothing else can be envisaged.

The point I am striving for is exceedingly difficult for us to get our minds round. I am not saying only that there must be a great deal that is unknowable by us. I am indeed saying that, but I am also saying that knowing itself, apprehending in any way whatsoever—the very existence of the possibility of any such category—is contingent on the apparatus we have for doing it, and can take only such forms as that apparatus makes possible. And not even only that, but also that the apparatus itself is contingent, an assemblage of physical stuff that occurred only because of the empirical circumstances that brought it about in the processes of evolution. If anything exists independently of us, then its very independence of us means that it does not exist in terms of the forms and categories that characterise the workings of the apparatus we happen to possess, an apparatus that we may even possibly be.

This being so, to conclude that nothing inconceivable can exist is an error. What can be conceived depends on our powers of conceiving, but what can exist does not depend on our powers of conceiving. The fact that we can apprehend only what the apparatus we have for apprehending can mediate is a fact about us and our powers of apprehension, not a fact about what exists independently of us. It means only that *we* can apprehend nothing else, not that nothing else can exist. *Anything* else may exist. But we have no means of contact with it. Just as, if no creatures had ever had eyes, the visual world would be permanently sealed off from any possibility of conceptualisation, so also is the existence of any and all of the worlds that would have been made available to us by the indefinitely large number of senses and mental capacities we might contingently have had but do not have. Any such worlds must be "there," just as the visual world is "there." And presumably they may be as close to us as our visual world is; but we have no apprehension of them.

Our technology can furnish us with enlightening indications of the way such things are. I happen to be writing these words in a bare, almost empty room, with no one else around. I am in an out-of-the-way house, and all around me is silence. Also all around me and up against me as I sit at my desk is empty air, empty space, which I look through as I look at the paper I am writing on. Yet radio technology, historically so recent, enables me to know that, in forms I have no way of apprehending with my body alone, the air around me is not empty or silent but full of music, played by symphony orchestras, jazz bands, and solo instruments, and full of voices talking simultaneously in English, Dutch, French, German and other languages. If I take a tiny transistor radio out of my pocket and switch it on I pluck all this and more out of the empty space around me. It is everywhere in the room, including between my eyes and the paper I am writing on. Every pair of lovers anywhere, murmuring with their noses an inch apart, have all this going on between their noses. It is everywhere all the time. And we know this. But without radio receivers we are without any means of "receiving" it ourselves, in which case nothing whatever seems to be there. Then what we apprehend is silence, nothingness. Before the recent concept of radio no human being seems to have envisaged anything like it or its possibilities, and yet the reality was always there. Today we can pick up radio signals from distant galaxies, signals that were "there" throughout the whole of human history. Goodness only knows what else is surrounding us without our having any notion of its existence.

    In the circles in which I have moved for most of my life a tendency to identify what is, or could be, with what human beings can know, or envisage, has been widespread. At Oxford I was actually told by a tutor of philosophy that the term "world" can mean either the totality of what exists or the totality of possible experience, the two being the same. But a logical distinction between the two must imperatively be made. When I myself taught philosophy at Oxford, one of the things I tried to do with all my students was get them to understand this. And it was difficult for them. Some never got hold of it—and these were among the cleverest of their generation. Something else that was difficult for all of us, including me, was to get our minds underneath and round the implications of it for the status of the world that we experience, the empirical world. We need to understand that what can be the case can go beyond the limits of the conceivable in an indeterminately large number of ways, each of which would constitute a realm to which even the inventions of our imagination could never reach. This makes demands of ultimate difficulty on our minds. Perhaps I should say, rather, that it makes demands of ultimate difficulty on our powers of intellectual imagination; for I have found that some people of the highest intelligence cannot meet these demands, which shows that they are not just intellectual. Those who meet them most naturally seem to be those who are also responsive to the arts— but there is no necessary connection between such responsiveness and intelligence. To many it seems that what is being said is unintelligible or bizarre or incredible, and in any case obviously false. The gift of intellectual imagination is as rare at all levels of academic life as it is outside academe. Most people, however intelligent they are, remain permanently unable to divest themselves of a compelling natural tendency to attribute us-dependent forms and categories to whatever exists independently of us. And it causes them to impute self-contradictions to anyone who makes the distinction.

To those who have understood my argument up to this point it will be clear, if it was not before, that only under bizarre and almost incredible conditions could everything that exists be apprehensible to us. One set of such conditions would be that everything that exists is itself created by mind, either our minds or a superior mind that subsumes ours—the mind of God, shall we say, a God who creates us and wires us up to the rest of his creation. Something recognizably similar to the first of these views was Fichte's, and something close to the second was Berkeley's. I find both of them audacious, and for that reason stimulating, exhilarating to think about—but incredible. Neither of them even attempts to explain the existence of that on which the existence of everything else is supposed to depend. The existence of God cannot be explained by the existence of God.

A different attempt at an explanation of why everything might in principle be knowable by us asserts that the apparatus we possess for understanding our environment has been developed interactively with that environment, through an evolutionary process that enables us to survive in it; and the very fact that we do survive shows that our knowledge fits reality, even if imperfectly. This claims too much. The evolution of our bodily apparatus has taken place without any contact with most of what we already know to exist—namely, outer space—and our bodies as they are would not be able to survive there. We are adapted for survival on the surface of this planet only, and would die in any other environment known to us, unless we were able to keep it at bay by encapsulating ourselves in an artificial bubble of man-made environment which we could carry about with us, like a deep-sea chamber, a submarine, a pressurised aeroplane or a spacecraft.

Among the claims that we can gain an understanding of everything with the resources we happen to have (plus those we are capable of inventing), the one that has the best chance of being true would hold that although our bodily apparatus has evolved without contact with most of already-known reality, and would be immediately destroyed by it, it so happens, by sheer coincidence, to contain everything we are ever going to need for an understanding of the rest. But even this has only to be stated for its implausibility to be self-evident, and its acceptance an unsupported act of faith. Logically it could be true. But logically we could never have grounds for accepting it. If it were true, it would be a coincidence coextensive with the cosmos. Its truth, though logically possible, is infinitely improbable, as well as being permanently unknowable. So I am driven to the view that total reality consists of some aspects that we are capable of apprehending and others that we are not.

That all living things are limited in their potentialities by what they are is obvious to human beings about any creature other than themselves. We find self-evident the inability of all the others, however intelligent, to understand more than a fraction of what we understand. We see, correctly, that each of them is enclosed in a world of possibility that its own nature makes available to it. A dog is enclosed in its dogness, its doggitude, and cannot get outside that. The cleverest dog that ever existed can do and understand only what it is possible for a dog to do and understand. Dolphins are amazingly intelligent, but how could a dolphin, in its aqueous universe, apprehend a fraction of what we know about the non-aqueous universe? Even the most creatively intelligent orangutan, an Einstein among orangutans, would not be able to master the principles of double-entry bookkeeping, or learn to read an orchestral score, or speak three human languages. Anyone who claimed of any natural creature apart from ourselves that it is capable, in principle, of understanding anything whatsoever would be talking obvious nonsense. Yet many assume this to be true of humans, and assert it explicitly. And many seem unable to achieve any real understanding of why it cannot be so. Yet the required understanding ought to spring from the reflection that human beings are a stage in the evolution of the selfsame animal kingdom as all other creatures belong to. But the validity of my argument is not dependent on that fact, if it is a fact. Whatever our origin, how could limitations imposed on us by our nature not be untranscendable? Yet if it is so, it almost certainly means that there are whole universes of unknowability for us, just as there are for dogs, dolphins, orangutans, and every other living creature. The sort of reasons why most of reality lies permanently outside the ken of a dog, a dolphin, or an orangutan apply by parity of reasoning to us.

It is essential to stress that this conclusion has been reached entirely through rational considerations. This has to be underlined because many people make contrary assumptions. Large numbers of people believe not just that total reality consists of what we know, or can know, and beyond that there is nothing, but also that to believe anything contrary to this is some sort of act of religious faith, or belief in the occult, or in the supernatural. Religious people themselves have a tendency to think this—to suppose that if you are not religious, then you believe that there is only the empirical world, whereas if you believe there is something more than the empirical world, you have a religious bent. Both are importantly wrong. Our argument is valid regardless of whether or not human beings are more than material objects, or God exists, or there is a spiritual realm of any kind. Our conclusions are such as any consistently rational person would find himself reaching. It so happens that I myself am agnostic about the existence of God, souls, and a spiritual realm, but even to say that is to throw a door open to irrelevance. In my own thinking the model for the unknowable that I most often use is the visual world as it exists for the congenitally blind, a visual world all round us all the time, with nothing "spiritual" about it, nothing religious, nothing supernatural, but just simply there. This, it seems to me, must be the situation all of us are in with respect to most of reality. Both religious and non-religious persons need to understand that a conception of reality as existing beyond the limits of apprehensibility is entirely rational.

For many people it is one of those insights that we are capable of acquiring with our heads while remaining unable to absorb them into our actual ways of looking at things, feeling about things, responding to things. There are many such truths. I know as I sit here writing these words that I am on the surface of a ball that is moving round the sun while rotating on its axis. This is the most basic of all truths about my location in space, yet I am unable to see it or feel it as being so, no matter how hard I try. I know that this brown wooden desk on which I write—so hard, so stable, so resistant—is made up of billions of colourless molecules that are in perpetual motion and consist of subatomic particles which are themselves in perpetual motion at speeds approaching the velocity of light; and that by far the greater part of the space occupied by the desk is empty space. But I am unable to go on for long relating in thought to the desk as so conceived: I keep slipping back into thinking of it as my familiar solid brown desk. I know that each of my friends and relations consists of meat, offal and bones not unlike those I might see in a slaughterhouse or a medical museum: a liver, a stomach, a heart, two kidneys, two lungs, a brain, skin, umpteen yards of intestine, a skeleton, and all the rest of it; but I find it almost impossible to see or think of them in that way for more than a brief experimental period; and I find it completely impossible to relate to them as so conceived. Most of the fundamentals of the human situation are like this. They are not self-evident, and in many cases they are so unobvious that a person who points one of them out for the first time becomes historically famous for doing so. The rest of us have no idea of their truth until such a person points them out. Even then we are unable to hold them in our minds for long as being as he tells us they are. Even so, what he says is true, and it remains true however little the rest of us understand astronomy, or quantum physics, or anatomy, and however little attention we pay to his revelations.

To my mind the most important single truth in philosophy is a truth of this kind, and is, as those are, without religious implications. It is the truth that, however difficult it may be for us to grasp, most of reality is unknowable by us, and—because beyond all possibility of apprehension—unconceptualisable.

SIX

Personal Reflections

FROM MY EARLIEST DAYS I WAS ABNORMALLY CURIOUS about what was going on around me—noticed it, absorbed it, remembered it. The absorption was marked by warmth and intensity of feeling; it was highly pleasurable, and I actively enjoyed it. Like a child at a circus, I was all the time being astounded by what I saw. It was astonishing as well as interesting, because it was there.

It was so evident that nothing could be taken for granted that I came naturally to question things, and questioning was a built-in part of the curiosity. Why did balls bounce, when nothing else did? Why did bicycles stay upright when moving but fall over the instant they stopped? What were the stars in the sky for? Why, in fact, was everything as it was, when it could just as well have been otherwise? Since I had this feeling so strongly I saw the way things are as being precarious, and not to be relied on. If I kept my eye on them, they would go on being the same, but if I turned away and then looked back, they might have changed.

Because I was always asking questions I was always having things explained to me. But unless I was already thinking along the lines of the explanations I found those surprising too. So I started trying to prepare myself for them. An aunt has told me that as a very small boy at the seaside, having just done some paddling, I asked her what the stones "at the bottom of the sea" were there for, and then, after a long silence during which she was unable to think of anything to say, I added speculatively: "I suppose they're to stop the water running out." When I started thinking in this way I must have realised that an explanation could be wrong. It cannot have been long before I realised that some of the explanations that were given to me by adults were wrong.

The first awareness I had of contact with a mode of being different from anything else was my awareness of music. I was struck into stillness by it, as if a dog or a horse had spoken to me. Although it came from somewhere else, a world different from this one, it was a peculiar kind of else-ness, because the experience was more direct and immediate than ordinary experience. The else-ness was a this-ness. It was as if the inside of things was talking to me. The outside had come off, as it were, and what had previously been inside was hidden no longer, and was communicating itself directly. Whereas other communication was a putting of something into words, here was the something itself. In itself it had nothing to do with words. It was the element you existed in before you got to words. It was inner being.

After the age of ten, when I started being taken to grown-up theatre and opera, I came to associate that sort of experience not only with music but also with the best of theatre, especially opera and Shakespeare. Later, in my teens, I had it when I was reading poetry. I discovered that this was what the grown-ups meant by "art." I caught overtones of it in novels. Ever-increasingly I found myself in contact with a reality *inside* life, below the surface, invisible to the eye, but more powerful than what was visible, and more immediate, in direct contact with what was inside me.

The only subsequent experience to resemble it in any way was sexual experience. The orgasms I started having at puberty had a lot in common with the experience of listening to music, but were if anything more intense. And they too were directly, unmistakably experienced as coming from outside the natural order of things. They were not of this world. They had suddenly, unaccountably crashed in.

Since what I am now attempting is the impossible task of conveying these experiences in words, perhaps

I ought to make it explicit that the experiences themselves were entirely non-linguistic. Not one of them
had anything to do with words, or could be satisfactorily captured in words—not even those associated
with works of art that were themselves in language,
like plays and poetry. My whole life I have experienced
the inexpressibility of such things directly, and I
know that attempts to communicate them always fail.
Feelings of real depth are bound to be non-linguistic,
given the crude inadequacy of language, and given
the more basic fact that it is only *from* experience that
concepts used about it in language can be derived
(which again must mean that the experiences themselves cannot be in language). Only thoughts and
feelings that are already familiar, or close to being so,
can come anywhere near being indicated in words.
The rest are untranslatable. In attempting to convey
them one struggles to apply inappropriate means to an
unattainable goal, hoping to achieve something that
can succeed, at most, in being better than nothing.

Uniquely specific, direct, non-linguistic experience
is the element in which we live, and it is radically
different from conceptual thinking, which can go on
only in universals. This is why works of art, embody-
ing as they do unique particulars and insights that
cannot be conveyed in words, and cannot be mir-
rored in conceptual thought, have their roots in lived
life and also cannot be translated. It is why, if someone responds to a work of art predominantly with his
intellect, he has already misunderstood it.

In my inner life, language was a late arrival. Until my early teens my interior world consisted of preoccupations and activities of other kinds, mostly sensory, emotional and physical. Language was where the world outside me began. If I wanted to communicate with anyone else, I had to put whatever it was I wanted to say into words, and then try to reach out to people through those. This was always difficult. There was a never-ending struggle with words. But everything that remained unspoken remained unconceptualised, so inside me there was still nothing between me and unique experiences. I was directly in amongst them, in them, *was* them, was my perceptions, and my responses to those, and my emotions, and memories, and feelings. They filled my consciousness and constituted my self-awareness. When I listened to music I *was* the music.

I still remember the not-entirely-welcome intrusion of concepts into this. They liberated me from near-total immersion in the present, thereby enabling me to do things I could not have done before; but at the same time they obtruded. Their abstraction and generality came between me and what would otherwise have been the uniqueness of the direct experiences, and blunted it. No longer was I unmediatedly up against experience, living it un-self-consciously, being it. Concepts got in the way, and made me self-conscious. Because they came between me and experience, experience was to that extent pushed off, so that I became ever-so-slightly distanced from it, though it still remained within. Since then I have lived with this doubleness, an awareness which is partly existential and partly conceptual, though by far the deeper and richer part of it is existential, preconceptual, prelinguistic. That is where music is, and the roots of intuition and insight, not blurred by the generalizing processes of conceptualisation. Only at this level is there unsullied understanding, though it is sometimes made difficult to get at by the intrusiveness of concepts. It must be from this level that originality and creativity make their way into our conceptually thinking minds—the derivative nature of concepts ensures that the basic movement can be only in that direction. Our profoundest intuitions, not only about art but also about people, relationships, emotions, morality, our conscious awareness, the living of life itself, are here. Most people see it as self-evident that such things cannot be adequately expressed in words, and there must be something impoverished about the inner worlds of those to whom that is not obvious. Like everyone other than them I have had to live my life with the problem that everything that matters most cannot be talked about. Not only is this true in all the examples I have given, it is also true of each individual's veriest consciousness of being alive, and the intimations this brings of realities other than our own, and the prospect of our certain death in this world. These things have being in our conscious awareness, but they cannot be formulated in concepts or expressed in words. We relentlessly drive language to do as much of the required work as we can make it do. We strive to get it as near as we can to what we would like it to say, and then gesture beyond it in what we feel and hope is the right direction. What we cannot get it to do is go all the way and embrace what we want to say—except, perhaps, in a work of art, and then it is not the concepts embodied in the words that convey our meaning but the work of art, which exhibits a meaning that cannot be stated.

I have lived all my life with an alive sense that consciousness transcends the material world. If this is so, the objects of consciousness *as we directly experience them* cannot be inertly material. The truth of this is at its most obvious with material objects that are human beings. Everything about my relationship with another person tells me that I am not having this relationship primarily with a material object. Primarily, it is a relationship with something else, as if there were something "inside" the material object. I put "inside" in quotation marks to remind both myself and the reader that it is a metaphor I do not think I am making contact with a something that occupies a space inside another person's body. What I am in contact with is something non-spatial to do with the unique personality and life of that person. And life, like consciousness, transcends matter. The person is, as it were, coming from somewhere "else" to meet me halfway (and I to him, or her). How different this is from contact between two material objects! Something similar is true of music, which has meant more

to me than anything other than people. Although material instruments are necessary to make sound, and
air is necessary to bring that sound to my ears, the
instruments and the air are merely media: the music
itself is not gas, or wood. And it too is met halfway by
something in me that is not material either. But I too
need physical media through which to engage with
it—I need ears and a central nervous system. These
also are no more the music than is the wood of the
violin. In our engagement with music, as in our engagement with people, something noumenal "inside"
us is directly in contact with something noumenal
"outside" us.

There are, I know, people who regard the whole
of reality including their inner lives (if they think
they have them) as being articulable in language.
Such people are inclined to think that if something
cannot be described, then that something is lacking
in definiteness, is vague. The truth is the opposite
of this. Existent entities, events and situations are
uniquely particular, as are all individual perceptions
and experiences. Since it is impossible for us to have a
separate word for each, words have to be of general
application to be usable at all. So it is our words that
lack specificity. People who believe that everything of
significance is expressible in language must be engag-
ing with life with the same generality as characterises
language. They are having their experiences in general terms. (It is noticeable what a high proportion of

scholars and literature-lovers are not especially interested in music.)

My first attempts to give expression to my deepest apprehensions of life arose from unconscious depths in the writing of poetry. I was foolish enough to publish some of it, and I regret that now, but what continues to interest me is that the poems came into my consciousness fully formed. Some of them were in conventional stanzas with lines that scanned and rhymed, but none of this had been worked out. The poems had constructed themselves in my unconscious mind and then revealed themselves to me ready-formed, just as my intricately plotted dreams at that time did. All I did consciously was write them down. Even more surprising to me now are some of the insights claimed by them. For instance, there is one in which these lines occur:

> For I believe (and now I speak
> Not for myself alone, but for you,
> For them that listen, and the whole
> Of inarticulate Man) that we create
> Eternity. We are not born
> With immortal souls: we must make them.
> To fail in this is to die. Most men
> Die. Hereafter-life is there
> For you to find, but must be bitterly
> Achieved. You cannot have Everything for nothing;
> It will cost you a lifetime of dying—living

And dying concurrently. Hence the sensitive
Fear, the fear of dying young, the fear
Of utter Nothing. To remain alive
And sane our need is luck, good fortune;
Justice is not in question.

I did not think this out. I did not *think* it at all. It just
came into my mind as it is, and I wrote it down.
Then, like any other reader, I had to read it to see
what it meant, and see if I understood it. And only
then did the question arise for me: "Is this true? It
starts 'I believe,' but do I actually believe this?" When
I wrote the poem at the age of eighteen I did not
know what the answer to that question was. But
there the lines were on the page in front of me, com-
pulsively articulated by a level of my self that my consciousness had never inhabited.

Today, as a mature adult, I cannot help remember-
ing in this connection Einstein's assertion that the
fundamental insights from which our scientific understanding of the world derives cannot be reached
by logical thinking or by observation, but only by
feeling *into* things (*Einfühlung*), intuition, acts of creation. As the reader now knows, I have come to regard this as true not only of the world as presented to
us by physics but of the ordinary world of our personal lives, including the realities presented to us by
the arts, and the demands of morality: in each case
the most important truths cannot be reached by any
amount of common sense or scientific observation,

nor by logical thought, but only by insights and intuitions that are driven forward by intense concentrations of feeling. Of these the question can always legitimately be asked: "But how can we be sure this is valid and not misleading?" At that point the whole armoury of critical appraisal should be brought to bear on them. But critical thinking alone, analytic thinking alone, cannot answer our questions. This was why those philosophers who believed that all philosophy ought to be analytic believed also that there were no genuine philosophical problems, only puzzles to be unravelled. "Not solved but dissolved" was their mantra.

In the view each one of us takes of reality, the way each sees and responds to things is conditioned by his personality, which is extraneous to the facts of the matter. The most familiar illustration of this is an optimist who, while drinking, looks at the bottle and thinks: "Oh good, it's still half full," at the same moment as the pessimist sharing the bottle with him looks and thinks: "Oh dear, it's half empty already." The two men confront exactly the same reality, and what each says about it is factually correct. So they agree on the facts. Yet the way they see the facts, and the way they respond to them, are almost opposite. We all have differences of this nature, in ways that can be a lot more subtle than my example. The worlds we feel ourselves to inhabit are different accordingly.

The philosopher from whom I have learnt most, Schopenhauer, is almost as different from me in these respects as it is possible to be. I have always felt that being alive is marvellous. I have consciously enjoyed being. Until I reached advanced old age, my attachment to life was so intense that I took it for granted that life on any terms was better than death. Readers might legitimately wonder whether I would have retained these attitudes if I had been struck down by a painful, chronic, incurable disease, or found myself in Auschwitz, but I honestly think I might. Some people in such circumstances did, and I inwardly believe that my younger self might have been such a person. Be that as it may, in the life I have actually lived I have always had an active sense that the world is miraculous, and that being alive in it is thrilling. Even life at its simplest has been vastly satisfying: just walking around and looking at things, meeting people, sitting about, eating, drinking, talking. Some of the greatest highlights of my existence have been not much more than intensifications of these activities: foreign travel, seeing the world at its most beautiful, exploring the great cities, meeting interesting people. This feeling for the miraculousness of life is a response not to this or that aspect of it but to the fact that it exists at all. *Existence* is the unbelievable thing. It is incomprehensible. Nothing could be an explanation of it—certainly not the existence of a God, which would then have to be explained, and there lies infinite regress. Existence as such, the fact of there being anything at all, is terminally inexplicable. What I feel about this is a double sense of wonder that the inexplicable is actual.

The inexplicableness extends beyond existence itself. Although one would not have expected anything to exist at all, if there had to be something, one would have expected it to be an arbitrary something, a chaos, a jumble, something that just *is*, a mess. But this is not so. All the natural objects round me are structured in ways that are intelligible. And not only their structure but a certain order between structures obtain to the outermost limits of the known material universe. Billions of heavenly bodies are known already to exist, and both in their internal structures and in their movements relative to one another there is an order so manifest and precise as to be expressible in mathematical equations, which enable us to make accurate predictions about their movements. Even more, we humans are made up of the selfsame physical stuff as they are: both we and they consist of atoms, and those atoms, again, have the same internal structure. It looks as if something ungraspably colossal is going on that has some kind of cohesion and identity, and is characterised by structures that are intelligible to the human mind.

The material world as I personally know it in my own little bit of it, the world in which I live my life, is so structured and ordered that it is comparatively stable. As I have said, I know it to exist only as the interaction between two incomprehensibles, an inaccessible me and an inaccessible reality that exists independently of me. But then the most extraordinary thing is that the world of interaction between these two unintelligibles is rationally intelligible. Reason holds sway there. And so far this alone has been its realm.

It is tempting to identify our conscious awareness with our sense of personal identity, but a little reflection shows this not to be so. We go to bed each night wanting to lose consciousness, but we certainly do not want or expect our identity to be suspended—if we thought this, we would be afraid of falling asleep. So although in our conscious minds we may equate our personal identity with consciousness, in the more capacious and consequential parts of us that lie below that level we understand that this is not so, and we are relaxed in that knowledge, and live comfortably with it. The intuition most of us have about the sanctity of individual human life can have nothing to do with the sanctity of consciousness. Even so there remains a particular magic about consciousness. After existence itself it is the most marvellous thing. Although the two are frequently confused, they are so radically distinct as to be disjunct. Most of what exists is without consciousness. We humans have direct knowledge, without understanding, of what consciousness is, but we have no grasp at all of what existence is: we understand neither what exists independently of us nor what we ourselves are.

When I try to put my experience of consciousness into words my bafflement is irreparable. Consciousness is what I most immediately have: I know it through and through—in fact it is only through it that I know anything else. I can describe what my consciousness is a consciousness *of*; but what the consciousness is in itself is inexpressible. The tiniest attempt to put it into words moves our focus away from it. And in so far as I am aware of the pure experience of being alive, it is this inexpressible awareness. As with existence it is impossible to imagine anything that could be an explanation of it. Perhaps, with such matters, we are no longer in the realm of *Why?*, or the realm of *How?* Perhaps they just *are*. It looks, after all, as if *something* just has to be.

However, that something is certainly not me. I do not have to be. In time, at least, it looks as if there was an unimaginably long period when I did not exist, before I was conceived. This suggests that I cannot take it for granted that anything of me will continue after my death. If it should happen that something does persist, it would be a stroke of incredible luck from the point of view of my present prospects. The future non-existence of my body is already a certainty, so anything of me that existed without that would have to be non-physical. What could that be? Could it, after all, be this miraculous, indefinable consciousness that I have? The fact of its regular suspension every night when I go to sleep makes its permanent suspension easy to envisage—the more so when I consider the evident dependence of it on my brain and central nervous system, both of which are doomed to disintegrate. If anything survives, it may have to be not just immaterial but also unconscious. This could well be unintelligible to me as I now am. In terms that I can comprehend, therefore, the odds seem to stack up against my survival. Nevertheless, survival does remain a possibility. It seems contrary to anything I can understand, though, whereas non-survival is a possibility I understand only too well.

This being so, I am afraid of death. What frightens me is the prospect of permanent oblivion. I do not need to have it explained to me that unchanging oblivion, in itself, cannot be frightening, because it cannot be anything. The point is that the *prospect* of it is frightening. It has terrified me all my life. To tell me that the situation will be the same as it was before I was born is to tell me an untruth. After my death oblivion will be the permanent extinction of what had once been a living and unique person, and nothing remotely like that was true of my pre-natal non-existence. It is the destruction of a full-bloodedly alive, conscious being that is so frightening for the conscious being. I find it strange that there are quite a lot of people who do not understand that.

I do find, however, that my fear of death decreases as the amount and quality of the life I would lose by it decreases. When I was younger, life was a feast, and I treated it as if I were a gourmet making his way from one banquet to another. In those circumstances the prospect of having this superabundance torn away induced panic. But now, in my eighties, life is no longer a cornucopia but something altogether more modest. The prospect of its being taken away is nothing like as distressing. When I was young, death meant the loss of a whole future, not only of my hopes, dreams and ambitions but also the actual life in all its abundance that I did in fact live in the decades ahead of me. Now there are no such decades. I have consumed them. For better and worse I have lived my life. By good fortune it has been a long one, containing a decent share of chances and opportunities, so I have little to complain about. Whether I made the best of it was up to me. If I did not, it was my fault. In the very living of that life the alternative confronting me has changed from that between death and an overflowingly full life to that between death and advanced old age. There is nothing like the same contrast. I am not claiming that I contemplate death with equanimity now—I do not. But there is no longer the sharp edge to my fear of it that there once was. This may seem paradoxical, given that I am so much nearer to it. But so it is.

If, in spite of my ignorance, I were compelled to gamble everything on what will happen to me when I die, I would come down on the side of oblivion, annihilation. If this is mistaken, as it might be, I think the most significant truth of all must be contained in the words of Schopenhauer: "Behind our existence lies something else that becomes accessible to us only by our shaking off the world." All my life my expectations have been torn between these two possibilities, but the former always had the stronger pull.

Whatever the truth may be, I find, and always have found, the inevitability of leaving this world uncomeable-to-terms-with. I have loved the world with inexpressible love. The very idea of its being torn away, never to return, is scarcely tolerable. And little though I understand death, one thing seems as near to being a certainty as almost anything in the future can be—namely, that when I die I shall no longer exist in this world. When I contemplate that, I feel not self-pity but a yearning *towards* the world, a longing for its continuance. Permanent separation from a life in it feels as close as anything can be to separation from everything. When I had an experience some years ago that I thought, while having it, was a stroke, and for a few seconds believed I was dying, the emotion that engulfed me was not primarily fear: it was primarily grief at the totality of loss—grief at the loss of everything.

SEVEN

Our Predicament Summarized

I KNOW THAT I EXIST, BUT I DO NOT KNOW WHAT I AM. Or rather, I do not know what "I" is. It could be just this physical object, my body, and its functions. If so, when the functions cease and the body dies—and is burnt to ashes which are then scattered—there will be no more me. Millions of my fellow human beings clearly believe that this is the way things are, some of them confidently and assertively. Millions of others do not. Among those there is a variety of differing views about what "I" really is. Some believe that there is an essential me that is not my body, and that it survives my bodily death—that each one of us has (no, is) an immortal soul. Others believe that we survive but not as individuals—that we merge into some sort of sea of existence, like a raindrop falling into the ocean. Others believe different things again. In each case there are intelligent and reflective individuals who hold the belief in question with tenacity and passion. Many have suffered torture and death for refusing to renounce it. If the inner sense of certainty and a commitment-unto-death of honest, intelligent people were a guarantee of truth, then all the religions of the world would be true. But they cannot be, because they contradict one another, so if one is true, there are others that have to be false. Only if we do not take them seriously can we assert that they are all true. At most one of them can be, and possibly none is.

What this situation illustrates, as clear as daylight, is that nobody actually *knows*. The plain fact is that I do not know whether I shall survive death or not; and nor does anyone else. I do not know whether I have a soul, and no one else knows either. To raise a possibly related question, I do not know whether there is a God, and nor does anyone else. From the fact that there are not grounds for an affirmative answer to any of these questions it does not follow that the negative is true. We have no definite knowledge of the negative either. A lot of people have unshakeable convictions in these matters, and are sure they know one way or the other, but unshakeable convictions are not knowledge.

At first it seems incredible that we human beings do not know what we are. It presents itself to our dawning realisation as an unfathomable mystery about the nature of our being. But on more rigorous investigation the key to the problem appears to lie not so much in the nature of our being as in the nature of our knowing. From the earliest days of philosophy there have been philosophers who contended this. The pre-Socratic Xenophanes wrote (translation by Karl Popper):

> The gods did not reveal, from the beginning,
> All things to us, but in the course of time
> Through seeking we may learn and know things
>   better.
> But as for certain truth, no man has known it,
> Nor shall he know it, neither of the gods
> Nor of the very things of which I speak.
> For even if by chance he were to utter
> The final truth, he would himself not know it.

The philosopher now most widely regarded as the greatest since the ancient Greeks, Immanuel Kant, argued in some of his profoundest pages that it is not possible for any sentient being to know its own nature. And there is now a strong consensus among philosophers of different kinds, including religious ones, that the existence of a soul, and of God, cannot be proved. Even among people who are not in any sense intellectuals it has come to be widely held that these are unanswerable questions, questions to which there must *be* answers, but answers which it is impossible for us to know. In the society in which I live I would say that if there is one view more than another that could be called the man-in-the-street's view, it would be this. So what I personally regard as the "correct" attitude is familiarly held, at all levels of sophistication from the most simple to the most subtle.

However, in whatever way one holds it, it is almost impossibly difficult to live by. Permanently facing the fact that we do not know what we are, or what future we have, if any, is something few of us seem able to do. Most, I believe, avoid thinking about it. As my father said when he knew he had the cancer that was soon to kill him: "One tries not to dwell on such things." Some, including many who cannot stop themselves from dwelling on such things, allow the natural strength of their desire for survival to push that desire from being a hope into some sort of watered-down belief which eventually modulates into a faith. They are correct in believing that it is true they *might* survive, and it is natural for them to want to with all their heart, so psychologically it is a short slide from what had been legitimate attitudes into believing that we survive. But the slide itself is illegitimate. As Freud once wrote: "Ignorance is ignorance: no right to believe anything is derived from it."

It used to be common, and was for centuries, for people to be congratulated on the strength of their faith, but I can think of no other context in which people are commended for the firmness of beliefs for which there is little or no evidence. There is nothing for congratulation in it. But, of course, leaders of sects of all kinds, political as well as religious, want followers who are like that.

It may be asked: If people find the real yet uncertain prospect of obliteration too terrifying to confront, why should they confront it? Why should they not evade it by not thinking about it, or by seeking refuge in a consoling faith? This question becomes harder for me to answer as I grow older. When I was young it seemed self-evident that we should try to live in the light of such truth as we can know, and I treated with contempt any suggestion that we might choose not to do that. Yet what about people who *cannot* face it? Should we insist on the destruction of their mental health? I do not think we should. I no longer believe in putting pressure on them to face more than they can bear. T. S. Eliot's words "human kind cannot bear very much reality" are among the most often quoted in the English language, and rightly so. I leave undisturbed anyone who does not want to think about these things, and I do not get into arguments about anyone's religious beliefs. But I do regard such people as no longer committed to the pursuit of truth. Let them preserve their equilibrium by all means, but let them not expect others to feel obliged to give active attention to whatever views they adopt for that purpose: consideration in the sense of tolerance and social respect, yes, but not consideration in the sense of investigative thought.

I am not writing like this from a position of supposed superiority. I used to regard commitment to

this kind of truth-seeking as the overriding value—
the need to discover, and live in the light of, as much
truth as we can find out about whatever it is we are—
and it is still how I would like to live as much as I can.
But I have discovered that there are things that I too
cannot bear. I have found in experience that whether
I like it or not I set a higher value on survival, certainly for others and probably for myself. If there is
something I cannot endure to contemplate, I no longer try to force myself relentlessly to contemplate it.
However, in that moment I know that I have opted
out of the pursuit of truth as my prime objective and
made survival my prime objective. There may be something biological and inescapable about the primacy
of such motivation, and in the last resort I do not
wish to change it, if only because that would be fruit-
less: understanding remains unachieved if we destroy
ourselves in pursuing it. What is desirable is to have
enough strength to face *sometimes*—not necessarily
in all moods or circumstances—what has to be faced;
and this is what I hope for. I have become a part-time
pursuer of this kind of truth, but alongside that a part-
time evader of it.

The chief trouble with evading is that the way one
thinks and lives then proceeds from the evasion, and
is shallow—not necessarily false but probably so, and
certainly without justification or integrity. One is living "as if" and hoping for the best, so there is something of pretence about one's doings, something acted,
and something rhetorical even about one's thinkings.

One is playing a game, though like many games it can be played with intense seriousness. If one lives like that all the time, one goes to one's grave without ever having *lived* seriously or intensely. One has only played, to get through the time while avoiding facing the reality of the situation. (This is the theme of what now appears as the emblematic play of the twentieth century, *Waiting for Godot.*)

As I have stressed, we had no say about coming into existence: we just woke up and found ourselves in a world. This world seems to consist, in its apparently irreducible features, of a "container" in four dimensions, three of space and one of time, whose contents are an indefinitely large number of material objects. Curiosity about the fundamentals of our situation naturally takes the form of interrogating them: what, we ask, is the nature of time, the nature of space, the nature of material objects; and what is the nature of us who find ourselves in this world, and the nature of our relationships to it, and to one another? Pursuit of these questions constitutes the mainstream of philosophy and its history, and it is out of this that the sciences have, one by one, emerged.

The sciences have been revelatory beyond anyone's expectations, and they continue to be so: in each generation they reveal things no one would have (or, often, could have) imagined previously. In the last hundred-and-something years they have transformed yet again our understanding of time, of space, of material objects, and of ourselves. However, not all the

knowledge that is available is available through science. Although science makes an indispensable con-
tribution to our understanding of the world we are
mistaken if we build, or try to build, our whole understanding of the world on it, or if we even imagine
such a thing to be possible.

If anyone makes a statement, it can claim to be
scientific only if other people can check it. For a long
time all science was believed to be concerned with the
observable motions of matter in space—even the so-
called social sciences, being about human behaviour,
were about observable motions of matter in space—so
scientific testing was seen as a disciplined and measured observation of things and their movements, and
of changes in those things and movements. In principle, such observations could be carried out by anyone.
Although no individual's observations could be relied
on to be one hundred per cent accurate, they could
be repeated and checked by others. So although scientific testing was never wholly objective, it was never
wholly subjective either: it was inter-subjective, pro-
ceeding by never-ending mutual criticism and correc-
tion. It was essentially a joint enterprise, a non-stop
journey directed at getting nearer the truth. Modern
science has become a good deal more theoretical,
more abstract than the science of the past, less exclu-
sively concerned with direct observation of material
objects; but the principle that our results must be re-
peatable by others still holds, and remains fundamental to valid claims to be scientific.

However, not all the knowledge that we as individuals have of ourselves is available to others. Yet we too are material objects. We may not be only material objects, but we are at least that—if the real us is nonmaterial, it is at least embodied—and that body is open to the investigations of science in all the ways that any other physical object is. But that does not account for all the knowledge of ourselves that we have. Each one of us is a material object that knows itself from inside. And this inner knowledge is unique to the individual. All sorts of things are going on inside me to which no one else has access—thoughts, emotions, reactions, memories, plans, hopes, fears, daydreams, a host of experiences of many differing kinds, and they are going on most of the time I am awake. My knowledge of these is direct, not mediated through the senses: that I have them is as reliable as any knowledge I possess. This is not to say that they are infallible. I can mis-remember, or be wrong about where the pain is, or mistake the nature of my own emotions. But in being fallible, they are no different from knowledge of any other kind—all knowledge is fallible, except possibly the immediate and *uninterpreted* experience I am currently having—and I am not sure even about that. No one can seriously maintain that only unimportant experiences are unique to the subject that has them. Our inner experiences include some of the most important we have—for instance, being in love, responding to Nature or to great works of art, and our deepest convictions about

morality and values. We can know as certainly as we
know anything that we have these experiences. Other
people, however, have only our word for it. I may lie
about being in love, or dissemble my moral convictions or my responses to works of art. Statements
about such things are not scientific, and I know of no
one who thinks they are; but they can be true, they
can be important, and they can be knowledge.

I am sometimes asked why, if I concede cognitive
validity to our responses to art, I do not extend it to
religious claims. The answer, broadly, is that in the
former case the existence of what my experiences are
a response to is not in doubt. If I react in a particular
way to a play or symphony, it is open to anyone to
deny the appropriateness of my responses but not to
deny the existence of the play or symphony. If someone tells me that he knows that God exists because
he has direct experience of God, I do not (usually)
question his sincerity, or question that he is having
an exceedingly powerful experience; what I question
is the interpretation he is putting on that experience.
He is claiming that because he has it he knows for
certain that a particular being other than himself exists; and this does not follow. He may be putting a
mistaken interpretation on his experience, something
all of us do sometimes—in fact, quite often. I doubt
whether he himself, if he is not a Roman Catholic,
would believe that people who sincerely claim to have
been in contact with the Virgin Mary have actually
been so, while most of the people who are willing to

accept such claims would not credit the truth of an equally sincere claim that someone had been in communication with a Hindu deity. These experiences are self-betraying in their culture-dependency. There seems to be always a predisposition to believe.

However, if, contrary to my disposition not to believe, it is the case that some of the claims of this kind are true, then it strengthens, not weakens, my point that it is a mistake to confine our attempts to understand the world to investigations of a scientific character. Even a world conceived of as the sum total of material objects includes all the human beings. And while scientific investigation of material objects can use only data that are available to all observers—what one might call "knowledge from without"—there is also a knowledge from within. It is indefensible to make no allowance for this in our attempts to understand the world—an arbitrary, unnecessary limitation, and a ridiculous one if our aim is to understand the nature of material objects, given that we ourselves are material objects. If there is, for each of us, a material object that he or she has direct knowledge of from inside, this must surely suggest the possibility that the most promising path towards an understanding of the nature of things lies partially within as well as partially without. In fact it seems self-evident. So I see our attempts to increase our understanding of the nature of things as embracing not only the sciences, which they must, and without inhibition, but also the arts, and philosophy as well, which concern themselves with other aspects of reality and experience. Unsurprisingly, they and the sciences have much in common. All of them are truth-seeking activities, open to everyone, penetrating beneath the surface of appearances and of accepted ideas, and providing us with a better understanding of how things are. All begin with speculative imagination, and rely fundamentally on intuition and insight, so that creative imagination plays a seminal role. But they also make indispensable use of criticism and self-criticism. And all are concerned to articulate and communicate their findings in coherent, publicly accessible forms. All carry their credentials with them, finding whatever justification they can have in outcomes: nothing can be said to be authentic or valid or true, and nothing beautiful, because an authority says so. Together they provide us with our deepest insights and most fundamental understandings, and this is indispensably because, among all those other considerations, they remain permanently open to radical questioning and criticism.

Not only are both our inner and our outer knowledge inherently fallible, they are also inherently limited in scope. The very first sentence of this summing up asserts that we do not know our own nature. The knowledge we have of ourselves from within tells us an enormous amount about ourselves, but it does not reveal to us our innermost nature—does not tell us what we ultimately are. In this respect the two forms of knowledge, inner and outer, do not differ. That is to say, our knowledge of other physical objects is also unable to reveal to us what *they* intrinsically *are*. In each case the ultimate subject and the ultimate object of our hoped-for knowledge remains uncognizable.

In the case of our knowledge of other objects one reason for this is that our apprehension of them is mediated by our senses as well as by our central nervous systems, including our brains, so that only forms of apprehension made possible by those media are available to us: perceptions, concepts and the rest. What things as they exist in themselves are independently of our us-dependent categories is something of which we can, in the nature of the case, form no conception. And apart from the fact that our knowledge of ourselves from inside is mostly non-sensory the situation there is a parallel one. What we can be directly aware of consists only of experiences. Therefore unless we *are* only our experiences—that is to say unless, as some people believe, there is no experiencing self that exists separately from experiences and has them—the self as it is in itself must remain forever unknowable. And that is the reality of our situation.

As I just noted there are people who think that if the so-called self can never be an object of direct knowledge to itself, we do not have adequate grounds for believing in its existence. All we know ourselves to be, they say, is our experiences—in which case we are, in Hume's words, "a bundle of sensations." But I think this is a mistaken view, because it assumes that adequate grounds for believing in the existence

of something can take only the form of direct cogni-
zance of it as an epistemological object. This is not
the case. We can know *that* something exists without
knowing *it*. It may seem slightly flippant to give as
examples the fact that I do not know China but I
know that China exists, or I do not know President
Obama but I know that he exists: the logical distinction being illustrated here is crucially important for
all thinking. Logically, it is possible to know that the
self exists without knowing the self; and this is our
situation.

What endows us with knowledge that the self exists is our experience of agency. For most of the time
when I am awake I am active in the world, controlling
the movements of my body and using it to move
things around. I consider alternatives, make choices,
take decisions, and then sometimes change my mind.
And I feel morally responsible for the consequences of
these actions. Even when I wish I could avoid doing
this I cannot. If this conviction of moral responsibil-
ity, unwilling as much as willing, is valid, it presup-
poses that the responsible "I" is continuous over time,
and is the same "I" as initiates action. So the experience I have of being myself does not consist only of
perceiving and knowing, it consists also of acting,
and experiencing the moral consequences of my actions. Through these I know myself to be a persisting
self who is a proactive moral agent—and this is in
addition to being a recipient of morally neutral experiences. It means that any account of "I" needs to be

an account not just (and perhaps not primarily) of a knowing subject but also of a moral agent.

My overall situation, then, is that I know that I have a persisting self for as long as I am in this world, but I am unable to fathom its inner nature, and I have no idea what happens to it when I die.

Not surprisingly, many people react to being in this situation by saying that if reliable answers to these most fundamental questions are unattainable, we ought not to waste time looking for them. However important the questions may be in themselves, it seems obvious to such people that if we know from the beginning that any enquiry into them is going to arrive at no satisfactory conclusion, then from the outset we know that the search is going to be futile and frustrating—so why embark on it? I have sometimes felt like this myself. Nevertheless I do not think it is an attitude that fits the reality of the situation. There is a tradition within Western philosophy that has irradiated these questions with light, even though it has not, and cannot, provide them with definitive answers. This tradition began with Locke, proceeded through Hume, and reached its highest development in the works of Kant and Schopenhauer. (Interestingly, Schopenhauer himself saw this line of succession as one single, continuing discussion: "It will be seen that Locke, Kant and I are closely connected, since over a period of almost 200 years we carried forward the gradual development of a coherent, consistent and uniform train of thought. David Hume may

also be considered as a connecting link in this chain.")
Anyone who has immersed himself in these philosophers is likely to have acquired a degree of illumination that he would not have achieved alone, unless he
were possessed of their combined genius. What the
study of this kind of philosophy gives us is not answers but insight and enlightenment.

These philosophers had a marvellous grasp of what
the fundamental problems we face are, and understood them to exceptional depth. They were good at
seeing which are interconnected, and what the connections are, while at the same time identifying apparent connections that are illusory or misleading.
They were able to envisage alternative solutions, and
see what objections could be brought against those,
and find that some of them did not survive rigorous
examination—and understood the implications of
this for the remaining apparent possibilities. Working
their way methodically, by analysis and argument,
through utterly basic questions, they functioned as
identifiers and excavators of what can be offered by
way of answers; and through that they became map-
makers of what is intelligible, identifying the bound-
aries of meaningfulness. They mapped out metaphysics. And because its questions are not questions to
which we can expect even straightforward answers,
let alone definitive ones, the study of them does not
provide us with knowledge as knowledge has been tra-
ditionally thought of—namely, justified true beliefs. It
is this that causes many people to regard metaphysi-

cal questions as not worth studying. But knowledge in the traditional sense is not available; and even if it were, it would not be the only precious possession a mind could have: there are also insight and enlightenment. Our understanding of the human situation—what is sometimes called the human predicament—is transformed by such studies. And so, therefore, is our understanding of the lives we ourselves are living, and hence our understanding of ourselves. Some of us feel compelled by something that Socrates put into words as "the unexamined life is not worth living." The investigation is indispensable to us, because our quality of life is so different with it from what it is without. And so is the degree of our self-understanding and self-orientation. We may not know where we are, but there is a world of difference between being lost in daylight and being lost in the dark.

In any case none of us can cope with life in this world if we throw up our hands in helpless bewilderment and passivity. We cannot avoid taking action, doing things—and whatever actions we perform require us to make decisions, and these involve choices. A choice can be made only with reference to a criterion, even if it operates unconsciously. So we do in fact have, and have to have, standards and values, whether we are aware of them or not. These have huge practical effects on our lives, however little we consider them. This being so, the more aware of them we can make ourselves, the more self-aware we can be in the use we make of whatever freedoms we have.

However, we find—as we do when we attempt to justify our knowledge of ourselves, or our knowledge of external objects—that when we enquire into our values, including our morals, we are unable to establish them on secure foundations. We may care passionately about morality, and assert value judgements, but when challenged to provide justifications we cannot do it in a way that precludes dissent. Because this is so, different people have different views of what the basis of morality is. Some believe it to be the will of God: they think there is a creator God who made us and requires us to behave in certain ways, and will punish us if we do not. There are others who believe there is no God, so our morality cannot have God as its source. Among those there is disagreement. Some believe that morality consists of rules framed by human societies for their self-preservation and well-being, others that its origins go further back into the biological processes of evolutionary animal development. There are other views too. And it is not the case that the different groups merely drum up alternative sets of supporting arguments for the same moral judgements. The moral judgements themselves can be radically different. To give only one example, Roman Catholics in our society regard abortion as murder, whereas millions of people in the same society see no moral objection to it. If such fundamental differences about morality exist even within our relatively homogeneous and stable society, what scale of differences ought we to expect elsewhere?

When we turn to aesthetic values the absence of demonstrable foundations is just as marked. It may be as obvious as anything can be that Schubert's most loved songs are better than songs composed by me, but it is not something anyone can prove. Even its obviousness obtains only because I have rigged the example. It is not obvious that Beethoven's piano concertos are better than those of Mozart or Brahms, and the subject is one on which music-lovers hold conflicting opinions. For thousands of years it has been recognised that there is no way of settling such disputes. A proverb to that effect was current among the ancient Romans: *de gustibus non est disputandum.*

So in everything that is most important to us— the nature of our inner selves, and also of other people's inner selves, and whether these selves have any lasting future; the nature of the world outside ourselves, the nature of space, the nature of time, the nature of objects in the world; our moral convictions; our responses to great art—we do not know the answers to our most fundamental questions. Such knowledge is not attainable, because we cannot put whatever ultimate beliefs we have on foundations secure enough to make them demonstrable. In such matters we never *know.* And because we do not know, conflicting beliefs are inevitable if there are going to be any beliefs at all.

It is easier to accept the security of a faith, either in the existence of unknowable entities or in their non-existence, than it is to confront the full range and scale of our ignorance and live with that. This last is what more than anything I would like to do—that, and perhaps to push back the frontiers of ignorance, as the philosophers I have named did in such fruitful ways. I am not in their class and have no secret, mad illusion that I am; but in the same way as Locke has become known as *the* empiricist among philosophers, and Hume as *the* sceptic, and Schopenhauer as *the* pessimist, I would choose, if I were to merit a tag, to be known as *the* agnostic. What I find myself wanting to press home more than anything else is that the only honest way to live and think is in the fullest possible acknowledgment of our ignorance and its consequences, without ducking out into a faith, whether positive or negative, and without any other evasions or self-indulgences.

Since we cannot live without applying or presupposing standards and values, the best way to engage with those is not as faiths or ideologies but provisionally, as being open to criticism both from ourselves and from others, and open to revision in the light of experience as well as criticism. Locke put it succinctly: "Where is the man that has incontestable evidence of the truth of all that he holds, or of the falsehood of all he condemns, or can say that he has examined to the bottom all his own, or other men's, opinions? The necessity of believing without knowledge, nay often upon very slight grounds, in this fleeting state of action and blindness we are in, should make us more busy and careful to inform ourselves than constrain others." It would have been better if Locke had talked not of "the necessity of believing" but of the necessity of provisionally assuming, the inescapability of "as if." We have no choice but to live and act on what we are right to call "the best of our knowledge" and the best of our judgement; but far from *believing* these to be true, we need always to keep in mind the fact that they may not be—and this is incompatible with *believing* them. They are necessary only as assumptions, and then only provisionally: and we have to keep a critical eye on them, and be always willing to change them.

From the fact that in all the areas we have been considering there can be no such thing as conclusive justification of our views, it does not follow that one view is as good as any other. All are open to testing against experience, and to criticism; and they stand up differently to such tests. Most of them, in the long run, do not stand up at all. So when I say that certainty is not available, I am not, repeat not, a relativist: I advocate that our assumptions, values, standards, morals and tastes should be never-endingly subjected to criticism, and should be revised or abandoned in the light of that criticism; and we should continue to entertain only those that stand up to this treatment. It means that although we cannot achieve certainty, we can, and do, make progress, because we can have very good reasons for changing from one view to another, and then preferring the new one to the old. It is this that causes the quality of our lives to be transformed by our involvement with ultimate questions. It also means that although I do not believe conclusive knowledge to be attainable, I am not what is normally meant by a sceptic, because I see us as never-endingly making improvements to our inherently provisional knowledge. This process of improvement has a prodigious practical application, and my attitude to the prospects of its continuance is optimistic.

For hundreds if not thousands of years people have been seeking secure foundations for their most important beliefs. In Western thought the search became highly intensified with Descartes—in mathematics, in logic, in science, in philosophy. It is extraordinarily difficult to get people, including oneself, to give up this long-established pursuit of the unattainable. The aggregate of false assumptions on which that pursuit rests is something that has been dubbed "justificationism." It consists of assumptions (1) that there needs to be positive justification for our beliefs, most obviously in science, if they are to be seriously held; therefore (2) that until we can produce such positive justification, at least for the most important of our beliefs, we do not have defensible grounds for holding them (from which some people infer that, until such time, we cannot rule out any alternatives); and therefore (3) we need as a matter of urgency to seek and find such justification in order to establish both the validity of the beliefs and our own justification for holding them. Each one of these statements is false.

The corresponding truths are that no justification of the kind we are talking about exists, and luckily for us we do not need it: although it is not possible to provide rational justification for believing in the truth of a theory, it is possible to provide rational justification for preferring one theory to another. So rationality requires us to renounce the pursuit of proof in favour of the pursuit of progress. In this way we can outgrow the need for conclusive justification without lapsing into either relativism or scepticism.

If we did not die, the unending inconclusiveness that results from this would not represent a problem for us: on the contrary, it would correspond directly to our situation. Our special problem derives from the fact that we do die—and that when we depart from this world we shall be in the same state of ignorance and uncertainty as we have always been in. What will happen to us then? Even those of us who, when the time comes, know ourselves to be at the point of death will not know the answer. I can only hope that, when it is my turn, my curiosity will overcome my fear—though I may then be in the position of a man whose candle goes out and plunges him into pitch blackness at the very instant when he thought he was about to find what he was looking for.

INDEX

abortion, 122
absurd, in existentialism, 56
aesthetics, 47, 88–94, 113–14
    language of, 90–92
    value judgements and, 28–29,
        50–51, 122–23
afterlife beliefs, 21, 22, 66–68,
    101–6
agency, 118
agnosticism, 124–27
    religious belief and, 23–26,
        114–15
anthropomorphism, 25
"as if" notions, 63, 101–3, 110,
    125
asteroid collision, 5

bats, 70
Beckett, Samuel, 111
Beecham, Thomas, 40
Beethoven, Ludwig van, 123
belief, 16
    commitment to, 52–53
    Hume on, 117–18
    knowledge and, 22–26, 113
    Locke on, 125
    predisposition towards, 115
    See also religious beliefs
Berkeley, George, 80
biochemistry, 14
blindness, 43, 59–60, 62–63,
    124–25

congenital, 20–21, 60, 68,
    83–84
Boadicea, 18
Brahms, Johannes, 2, 123

causality, 19
Chomsky, Noam, 27, 40
colours, 21, 63, 74–75
common sense, 12, 67
conceptualisation, 72–74,
    91–92
consciousness, 36, 40, 47, 54,
    100–102
    conceptualisation of, 92
    personal identity and, 49, 99,
        100, 105–7
    Schrödinger on, 68
    sleep and, 95, 100, 113

death, 12–13, 95–96, 98
    afterlife and, 21, 22, 66–68,
        101–6
    beliefs about, 107–8
Descartes, René, 126
dogs, 81–82
dolphins, 81
Dostoevsky, Fyodor, 51
dreams, 95, 100, 113

Einstein, Albert, 8–11, 96
Elgar, Edward, 45
Eliot, T. S., 109